. P8M92

THE PSITTACOSIS GROUP
AS BACTERIA

C I B A   LECTURES IN MICROBIAL BIOCHEMISTRY

THE PSITTACOSIS GROUP AS BACTERIA

BY JAMES W. MOULDER

1964

JOHN WILEY & SONS, INC.

New York · London · Sydney

The CIBA Lectures in Microbial Biochemistry were established in 1955 at the Institute of Microbiology, Rutgers, The State University of New Jersey, through the support of CIBA Pharmaceutical Products Inc., Summit, N. J. The lectures are given in the spring of each year at the Institute of Microbiology, New Brunswick, N. J.

PREFACE

I wish to thank CIBA for generously providing the opportunity to visit the Institute of Microbiology at Rutgers in May 1963 and to present the three lectures on which this book is based. I particularly want to thank the members of the Institute for their kind hospitality which made my visit a most pleasant and stimulating one.

The following journals have kindly allowed me to reproduce figures from publications of my research group: *Journal of Infectious Diseases* (Figures 2, 5–12, 23), *Journal of Bacteriology* (Figures 24, 28), and *Annals of the New York Academy of Sciences* (Figure 15). Drs. A. Tamura and N. Higashi graciously permitted me to use some of their data which were unpublished at the time these lectures were given.

J. W. MOULDER

Department of Microbiology
The University of Chicago
January 1964

CONTENTS

GENERAL PROPERTIES
OF THE PSITTACOSIS GROUP

Man has known for almost 100 years that he occasionally contracts pneumonias from exotic birds.* The disease was named psittacosis in recognition of its frequent association with parrots (Latin *psittacus*) and was for a while erroneously attributed to infection with a *Salmonella*. However, psittacosis remained a rare and obscure disease until the pandemics of 1929 and 1930 involved 12 countries and 800 cases. Just at the termination of the pandemic, brought about by strict regulation of shipment of parrots from tropical countries, Levinthal, Coles, and Lillie almost simultaneously reported the presence of minute, spherical, basophilic bodies in reticuloendothelial cells from infected individuals. Two years later, Bedson and Bland proved that these bodies were the etiologic agents of psittacosis. Subsequent work by Bedson and his associates (reviewed by Bedson [2]) demonstrated that the agent of psittacosis was a

* For a full account of the early history of psittacosis, see Meyer.[1]

new kind of infectious entity, not immediately identifiable as either virus or bacterium. We now recognize the psittacosis agent as the type species of a large group of organisms infecting man, other mammals, and birds, which for want of a more suitable name I shall call the psittacosis group of microorganisms (see Weiss [3] and Wenner [4]). As summarized in Table 1, the group is defined by an obligately intracellular way of life in which multiplication proceeds by means of a unique developmental cycle, by a common

TABLE 1

The Psittacosis Group of Microorganisms

Common Characters That Define the Group	Specific Characters That Define Individual Agents
Particle morphology Developmental cycle Group antigens	Specific antigens Virulence for different hosts Pathology of the natural disease

Some Important Members of the Group

Avian Agents	Human Agents
Psittacosis Ornithosis	Lymphogranuloma venereum Trachoma Inclusion conjunctivitis Human pneumonitis

Mammalian Agents

Meningopneumonitis Mouse pneumonitis Feline pneumonitis	Bovine enteritis Bovine encephalitis Enzootic abortion of ewes Sheep pneumonitis

References 3, 4.

morphology of individual particles, and by a common antigen. Individual agents are identified by their virulence for different hosts, by the pathology of the diseases they produce, and by the possession of specific antigens. Although these organisms produce very different diseases in their natural hosts, they behave more or less alike in experimental animals, chick embryos, and cell cultures, so that results obtained with one agent-host system may often be cautiously applied to the entire group. To avoid tiring repetition, I shall frequently not identify specific host-agent systems when the findings appear generally applicable to the entire group.

Members of the psittacosis group are transmitted from one vertebrate host to another without intervention of an arthropod vector. Popular conceptions to the contrary, natural infections are seldom acute and are frequently characterized by long periods of latency. Infection may occur in young animals with little mortality or overt sign of disease. The host recovers, but the parasites persist in a potentially virulent form, ready on the proper occasion to initiate a frank infection in the original host or to be transmitted to a new one.

In this book, I shall maintain the thesis that the strict intracellular parasites of the psittacosis group are descended from bacterial ancestors without such restriction in habitat, and that their relation to the bacteria is so close that, begging taxonomic subtleties, they are bacteria. In this chapter, I shall describe the multiplication of these microorganisms in infected cells and the chemical composition of isolated particles, while in the next I shall discuss the metabolic properties of the psittacosis agents. Finally, I shall summarize my ideas on the basic biochemical properties of these microorganisms and on their relationship to other forms of life.

The Growth Cycle of the Psittacosis Group

When observed in the electron microscope, populations of psittacosis group agents are heterogeneous in size and internal structure. Figure 1 is a group of air-dried and metal-shadowed particles, greatly distorted in process of preparation for electron microscopy. However, it is still apparent that no two have the same diameter, length of shadow, or central structure. Figure 2 is an electron micrograph of a thin section through an infected cell, in which artifacts are at least held to a minimum. The great variability in size is again evident, and the diversity in structure of the electron-dense central body is particularly obvious. However, in spite of this continuous morphological spectrum, it is a convenient approximation to regard psittacosis group populations as being composed of two main particle types: one relatively small and with a dense central body, the other relatively large and with no central body.

As a second approximation, the complex and still imperfectly understood developmental cycle of the psittacosis group may be regarded as an orderly alternation of the two particle types, as shown in Fig. 3. The growth cycle is normally initiated by a small particle which is specialized for a brief extracellular journey and invasion of a new cell. Its genetic material is sequestered and protected for this hazardous trip. Hence, it multiplies neither in the cell in which it is formed nor in the cell which it invades. It must undergo a long internal reorganization into a large particle before multiplication can begin. The large particle is the vegetative form of these microorganisms. It is specialized for intracellular multiplication by binary fission, survives poorly extracellularly, and is rarely able to invade a new cell. The growth cycle is completed by the reorganization of a portion of the large particles into a new generation of

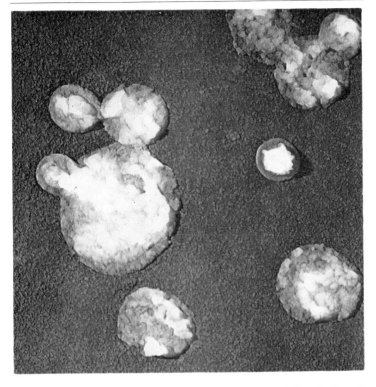

Fig. 1. Meningopneumonitis agent concentrated from infected allantoic fluid. Dried in air and chromium-shadowed ($\times 25,000$). Reference 19.

small particles to yield a mixed terminal population consisting of varying proportions of the two particle types.

Growth Curves. This idealized developmental cycle is derived from many closely spaced observations on a number of agents growing in several different host cells. One-step growth curves may be obtained in cell culture by standard procedures or in the chorioallantoic ectoderm of the chick

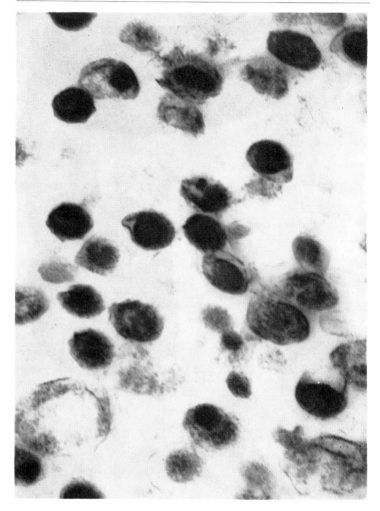

Fig. 2. Psittacosis agent (strain 6BC) in Chang's human liver cell 45 hours after infection. Thin section of osmium-fixed and methacrylate-embedded material (×50,000). Reference 7.

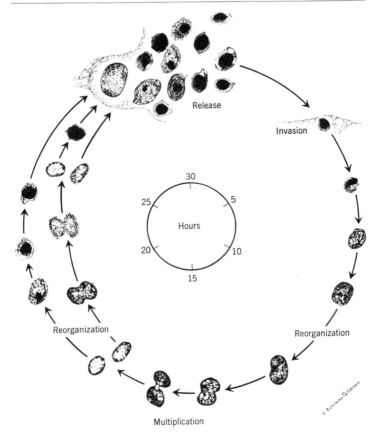

Fig. 3. Idealized representation of the growth cycle of the psittacosis group.

embryo by infecting virtually all of the available cells with the initial inoculum, thus leaving no susceptible cells for secondary cycles. Figure 4 shows the growth of the agent of feline pneumonitis in the chorioallantoic ectoderm and is

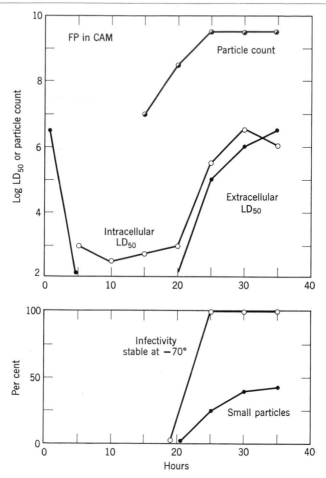

Fig. 4. Growth cycle of the agent of feline pneumonitis in the chorio-allantoic ectoderm of the chick embryo. References 5, 6. $10^{6.5}$ LD_{50} of agent were inoculated on the chorioallantoic ectoderm of a 9-day-old embryo. Infectivity was determined in chick embryo yolk sac. Particle counts and per cent small particles were determined by electron microscopy of supernatants from disrupted membranes.

based on the work of Litwin.[5, 6]   The growth curve may be divided into an early and late phase, with the dividing line drawn at 20 hours after infection.   In the early phase there is no extracellular infectivity, the intracellular infectivity is completely destroyed by brief storage at -70 C, and subpassage results in an abnormally lengthened cycle of 90 hours.   Since the low order of infectivity observed in the early portion of the growth cycle is qualitatively different from that seen later, it is probably due to the feeble infectivity of the large particles and not to unadsorbed inoculum.

At about 20 hours, extracellular infectivity appears, storage at -70 C no longer destroys infectivity, and subpassage gives a normal cycle of 30 hours.   All these changes coincide with the appearance of the small dense-centered particles in the population.   This conclusion is supported by examination of the late phases of the growth cycles of three other agents, one in two different hosts (Fig. 5).[7]   In each system the 15-hour population consisted entirely of large particles, and shortly thereafter, chick embryo infectivity, total particle count, and the proportion of small particles in the population began to rise rapidly.   Small particle formation was initiated at slightly different times in the different systems, but once begun it proceeded at the same rate.   In each example, the sharp rise in infectivity that marks the beginning of the late phase of the growth cycle began at the time when small particles could first be detected.   It may be concluded that the early phase is that portion of the growth cycle in which only the large vegetative particles are present, and that the late phase begins abruptly with the first appearance of the small particles with their greater stability and infectivity.

Electron Microscopy of Infected Cells.   This interpretation of the growth curves is supported by electron microscopy of thin sections of infected cells, a technique which allows the

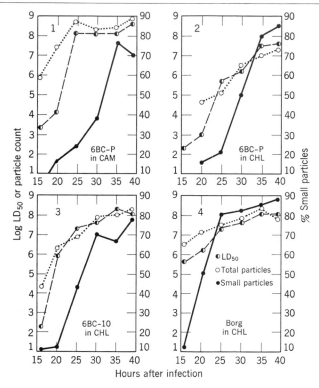

Fig. 5. Late phase growth curves for three different psittacosis strains. CAM = chorioallantoic membrane. CHL = Chang's human liver cells. 6BC-P = psittacosis agent (strain 6BC), egg-adapted. 6BC-10 = psittacosis agent (strain 6BC), CHL-adapted. Borg = psittacosis agent (Borg strain). Reference 7.

direct examination of intracellular populations.[6, 7] Three small particles were apparently caught in the act of entering a host cell in Fig. 6. Little is known about the process of invasion except that with well-adapted, vigorous agents, it is both fast and efficient. Absorption is measurable within

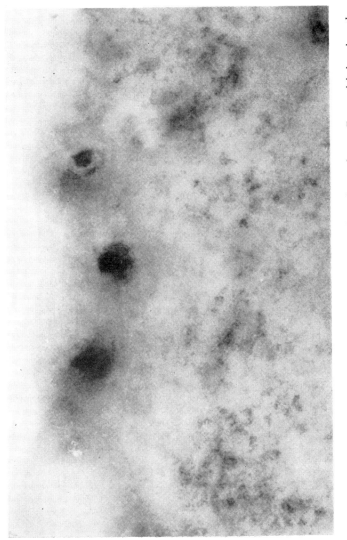

Fig. 6. Feline pneumonitis agent entering a cell of the chorioallantoic ectoderm. Frozen-dried and methacrylate-embedded (×45,000). Reference 6.

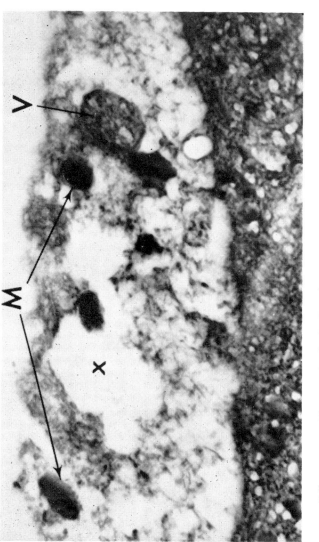

Fig. 7. Feline pneumonitis agent in chorioallantoic membrane 10 hours after infection. Frozen-dried and stained with platinic tetrabromide (×22,000). V = agent particle. M = mitochondria. Reference 6.

minutes and complete within an hour.[8,9]   Comparison of the total particle count with the chick embryo infectivity in Fig. 5 reveals that in the terminal populations of these highly infectious psittacosis agents, the ratio of particles to chick embryo infectivity approaches unity. This level of efficiency suggests a specific interaction between the agent and the invaded cell, because a passive, nonspecific penetration would not be expected to yield a one-to-one ratio between total particles and infectious units. With weakly infectious members of the group, such as the trachoma agent, the particle/LD_{50} ratio may be nearly a million.[10]

One to 10 hours after infection, numerous intracellular bodies of about the size and structure of large particles may be seen in the cytoplasm of infected cells, but they cannot be unequivocally identified as particles of the infecting agent. Application of the ferritin conjugated antibody technique[11] would be especially valuable here. By 10 hours, clearly recognizable agent particles are present (Fig. 7). They are easily distinguished from mitochondria, the only other cytoplasmic particles in the same size range. They have the size and internal structure of large particles, they are in close association with the cytoplasm, and they have not yet begun to multiply.

At the onset of multiplication 12 to 15 hours after infection (Fig. 8), the agent particles have a high intrinsic electron density, suggesting that a large amount of new cell material has been synthesized with little division, as in the lag phase of a bacterial culture. Many small inclusions may be seen, each a microcolony formed by multiplication of a single particle and lying in a cytoplasmic vesicle. Although light microscopists described a limiting vesicular membrane, no such structure is visible in electron micrographs. This is probably the time when these microorganisms are the most active metabolically, and it is most unfortunate that it is

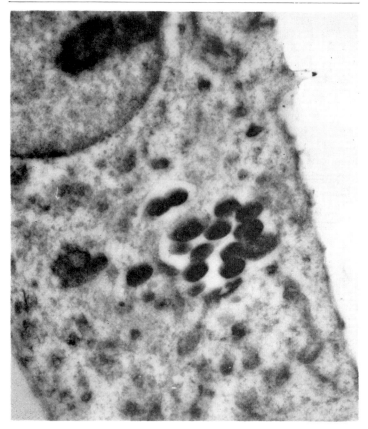

Fig. 8. Psittacosis agent (strain 6BC) in Chang's human liver cell 12 hours after infection. Osmium-fixed (×14,000). Reference 7.

virtually impossible to separate enough of the early phase particles from the infected cells to determine their enzymic capabilities.

Growth curves indicate that the maximum rate of multi-

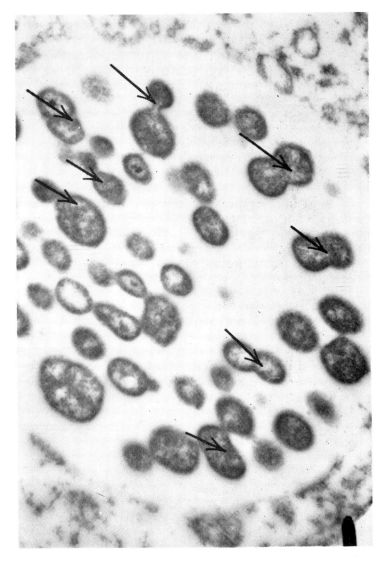

Fig. 9. Meningopneumonitis agent in Chang's human liver cell 20 hours. Osmium-fixed. Arrows indicate dividing forms (×14,000). Reference 7.

plication occurs 15 to 25 hours after infection, and it is at this time large particles in process of division are most numerous (Fig. 9). As the psittacosis group agents enter the logarithmic period of multiplication, their internal structure becomes less electron-dense, suggesting that multiplication is now outstripping synthesis. The cytoplasmic vesicle continues to enlarge as multiplication proceeds. Dissolution of the cytoplasm in the region of the inclusion could be brought about either by secretion of exoenzymes by the growing agent, or by the activation of lysosomal enzymes as suggested for viral infections by Allison and Sandelin.[12] Its fluid probably contains substrates of all degrees of complexity, and one may speculate that if the vesicle fluid could be reproduced in the test tube, in vitro growth of a psittacosis agent might well be achieved.

It is difficult to avoid concluding that the particles are multiplying by binary fission when a single section through one inclusion yields examples of almost every conceivable step in the process (Fig. 9). Some dividing structures are reminiscent of a budding yeast cell. In this higher magnification of a dividing particle (Fig. 10), the daughter cells have almost completely separated and only a thin area of contact remains. Binary fission is, of course, a distinctly nonviral mode of reproduction.

Twenty hours after infection, about halfway through the period of most rapid multiplication, dense-centered particles begin to appear. Discussion of the difference between the two particle types is best deferred for the moment. Particles such as those in Fig. 11 were seen by Gaylord [13] and leave little doubt as to the origin of particles with central bodies—they are formed by reorganization of the large ones. The rare particles with two dense centers probably arise when one division takes place after formation of the central body begins. With these exceptions, particles with

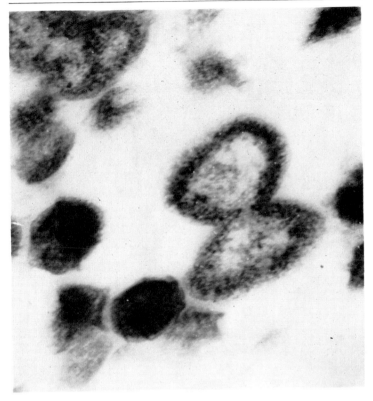

Fig. 10. Psittacosis agent (Borg strain) in Chang's human liver cell at 30 hours. Osmium-fixed (×56,000). Reference 7.

dense centers are never seen to undergo fission. Differentiation into small forms continues for several hours until, depending on the particular host-agent system involved, 30 to 90 per cent of the terminal population is of the small particle type, as in the large 30-hour inclusion shown in Fig. 12. The cell in which it lies is grossly distorted, the

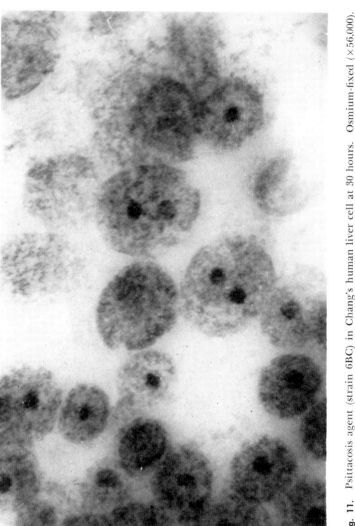

Fig. 11. Psittacosis agent (strain 6BC) in Chang's human liver cell at 30 hours. Osmium-fixed (×56,000). Reference 7.

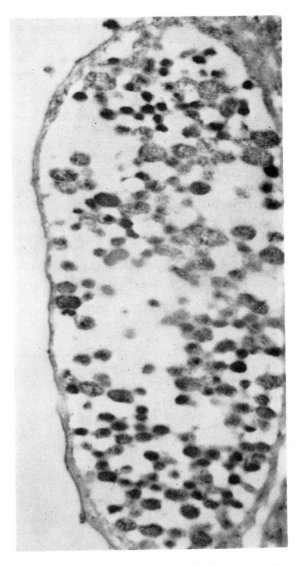

Fig. 12. Feline pneumonitis agent in chorioallantoic ectoderm at 30 hours. Frozen-dried (×17,500). Reference 6.

cell membrane is broken in several places, and many particles appear to have been released. However, nuclear damage directly attributable to agent growth is never observed, and infected cells may occasionally undergo normal mitosis and cell division.[14]

Let us return for a brief summary to the idealized growth cycle (Fig. 3). It may in many respects be analogized to the bacterial growth curve. There is a long lag period in which the particle increases in size but does not divide, a period of logarithmic multiplication by means of binary fission, and a stationary period in which further multiplication does not occur. It is tempting to carry this idea further by analogizing the formation of small particles with the process of bacterial sporulation. However, the small particles have none of the distinctive properties of bacterial endospores. The alternation of particle structure and function finds no ready parallel in the growth of bacterial cultures and represents a positive adaptation to intracellular life; that is, the appearance of new functions and an increase in the complexity of interaction with the environment.

Chemical Composition of the Psittacosis Group

Another way to study an intracellular parasite is to separate it as cleanly as possible from the host cell in which it has grown and to determine its chemical composition and enzymic potentialities.

Preparation of Agent Concentrates. In chemical investigations, we have worked almost exclusively with the agent of meningopneumonitis which, although noninfectious for man, grows to high titer in the allantoic cavity of the chick embryo and in certain cell cultures. Under appropriate conditions, new generations of agents are released from the infected entodermal cells lining the allantoic cavity with little release of cell debris. Several cycles of differential

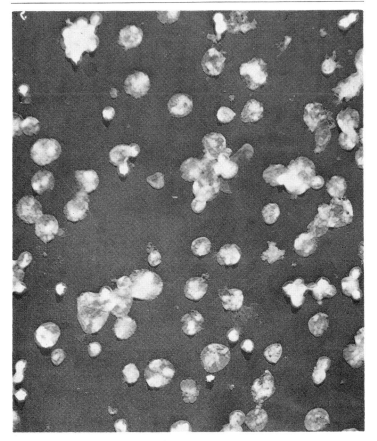

Fig. 13. Meningopneumonitis agent concentrated from infected allantoic fluid. Air-dried and chromium-shadowed (×5600). Reference 19.

centrifugation of infected allantoic fluid yield concentrates almost completely free of host-derived particles and with only slightly impaired infectivity, one chick embryo LD_{50} being equivalent to less than 50 particles.[15–17] Figure 13 is a typical electron micrograph of a meningopneumonitis concentrate. Many such electron micrographs were taken of each concentrate and used as the chief criterion of freedom from host material. The great heterogeneity in particle size and structure makes the application of more conventional measures of homogeneity a practical impossibility. Allantoic fluid concentrates contain the two particle types in a nearly constant ratio of two large to one small particle. Because of the great difference in size, more than 95 per cent of the mass of an allantoic fluid concentrate is derived from large particles. Thus, the properties of such preparations reflect mainly the contribution of the large particle.

In contrast, propagation of the meningopneumonitis agent in suspensions of Earle's L cells yields terminal populations consisting chiefly of the small particle type. Tamura and Higashi [18] have used sonic disintegration, digestion with trypsin, ribonuclease and deoxyribonuclease, and density gradient centrifugation of infected L cell supernatants to produce purified preparations made up almost exclusively of small particles. We have obtained similar results independently.[19] Figure 14 is an electron micrograph of one such preparation with a single large particle included in the field for sake of comparison.

Differences between Large and Small Particles. Both large and small particle concentrates were analyzed by means of the classical Schneider-Schmidt-Thannhauser phosphorus fractionation (Drs. Tamura and Higashi have generously allowed me to present their data on small particles). To the surprise of all concerned, the two sets of data were practically identical (Table 2). Phospholipid, ribonucleic acid (RNA), and deoxyribonucleic acid (DNA) were present in the same ratio in both kinds of particles. While more detailed analysis will be required before it can be positively concluded that the chemical composition of the two particle

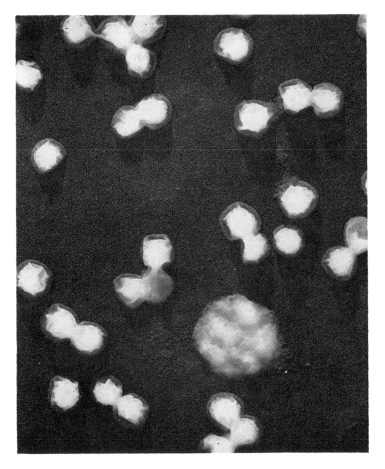

Fig. 14. Meningopneumonitis agent concentrated from L cells. Air-dried and chromium-shadowed (×23,000). Reference 19.

TABLE 2

Comparison of Large and Small Particle Preparations of Meningo-pneumonitis Agent: Distribution of Phosphorus in the Schneider-Schmidt-Thannhauser Fractionation

	% Total Phosphorus	
Fraction	Large Particle Preparation * 67% by count 95% by mass	Small Particle Preparation† 99% by count
Acid-soluble	10.8	7.2
Lipid	34.9	31.5
Ribonucleic acid	31.3	27.4
Deoxyribonucleic acid	22.5	26.6
Residue	2.7	4.1

* Reference 36.   † Reference 18.

types is the same, it appears likely that there are no major differences. Thus, these chemical findings support the conclusion drawn from morphological observations that one particle type may be transformed into the other. A simple explanation for the interconversion of large and small particles is that they differ mainly in degree of hydration and that differences in size and internal structure stem directly from changes in water content. Large and small particles should, according to this explanation, have markedly different densities. However, when mixed populations were centrifuged in continuous density gradients, the small particles sedimented only slightly faster than the large ones.[20] Also, if hydration and dehydration were the only process involved, it is hard to see why the intracellular transformation of an invading small particle into a multiplying large one should take 12 to 15 hours. It therefore appears that the interconversion of particle types is a more complicated phenomenon than a mere change in water content.

The key to the problem probably lies in the structure of the dense central body of the small particle. High resolution electron microscopy has so far failed to give a clear-cut description of its structure.[21-23] For a number of reasons, the central body does not appear to be homologous with the nuclear body of bacteria. The dense center becomes visible at the time cell division ceases; it is highly osmophilic whereas the nuclear bodies of bacteria are weakly osmophilic, less so than the surrounding cytoplasm;[24] and the nucleic acid may be extracted by hot deoxycholate without altering the electron density of the central body.[16] It seems more likely that the dense center of the small particle represents some unknown kind of aggregation which renders that particle incapable of division but which makes it more resistant to extracellular stresses. The nature of the differences between large and small particles and of the stimuli which trigger their interconversion remains a fascinating problem for future investigation.

Gross Chemical Composition. Table 3 gives the gross chemical composition of large particle preparations of the meningopneumonitis agent. There is a comparatively high proportion of lipid and a comparatively low proportion of protein and carbohydrate. The only remarkable thing about the agent protein is the total or almost total absence of arginine and histidine (see also Gogolak and Ross[25]). The carbohydrate content is low, possibly because of incomplete hydrolysis or destruction of sugar during hydrolysis. Of the small quantity found, a significant fraction is hexoseamine. Lipids are surprisingly high, comparable in level to that of the mycobacteria. Phospholipids of the lecithin type are present,[25] and cholesterol is undetectable. Better characterization of the lipids of these microorganisms is badly needed.

TABLE 3

Gross Chemical Composition of the Meningopneumonitis Agent

Constituent	% of Dry Weight
Protein	35
Hexoseamine	0.6
Reducing sugar	1.1
Deoxyribonucleic acid	3.5
Ribonucleic acid	2 to 7
Phospholipid	7.5
Cholesterol	0
Other lipids	40

References 16, 35.

Nucleic Acids of the Psittacosis Group. Both RNA and DNA are present. Dr. Pirsch has recently determined the base composition of the nucleic acids of the meningopneumonitis agent and of the chick embryo tissue in which it multiplied (Table 4).[26] The agent DNA is characterized by a very low guanine plus cytosine content (29.3 per cent), much lower than that of the host tissue. The base composition of the meningopneumonitis DNA is consistent with a double-stranded structure.

In light of interest in the base composition of DNA as a criterion of phylogenetic relationships, it may be noted that the guanine plus cytosine content of meningopneumonitis DNA is higher than that of the pleuropneumonia-like organism studied by Jones and Walker [27] (24.8 per cent) and lower than that of typhus rickettsiae (32.5 per cent).[28] The mean DNA content per particle is 7×10^{-16} gram, equivalent to a molecular weight of about 4×10^8. This is more than twice as much as for vaccinia virus [29] and about one-tenth as much as for *Escherichia coli.*[30]

The base composition of the meningopneumonitis RNA is not related to its DNA. Although it is very similar in composition to ribosomal RNA of bacteria, we have not shown the presence of ribosomes in the psittacosis group. However, indirect evidence for psittacosis group ribosomes is given by the inhibition of agent multiplication by chloramphenicol,[4] which several workers have shown to inhibit the synthesis of protein in bacterial ribosomes but not in those of vertebrate origin.

Although several different investigators have reported the presence of both DNA and RNA in purified preparations of members of the psittacosis group,[16, 18, 25, 31, 32] it has recently been claimed on the basis of acridine orange staining that these agents contain only RNA in the early stages of the growth cycle and only DNA terminally.[33] Since such alternation of nucleic acid type in different phases of the growth cycle of an infectious entity is without known parallel, this claim needs confirmation by other techniques before it can be taken seriously. Since viruses contain either RNA or

TABLE 4

Base Composition of DNA from Meningopneumonitis Agent and Chick Chorioallantoic Membrane

Preparation Analyzed	Moles per 100 Moles Base Recovered				Base Ratio of Dissymmetry
	Adenine	Guanine	Cytosine	Thymine	
Meningopneumonitis agent	35.2	14.3	15.0	35.4	2.40
Chorioallantoic membrane	28.4	22.7	20.3	28.4	1.32

Reference 26.

DNA and never both, the presence or absence of both kinds of nucleic acid in the psittacosis group becomes of fundamental importance in establishing their evolutionary heritage. The great discrepancy in base ratio between the DNA of host and agent concentrates immediately establishes the latter as a true constituent of the microorganism (Table 4).

The main point of contention is whether the RNA of agent concentrates made from terminal populations is of agent or host origin. Some time ago, we offered two different kinds of evidence that it is agent RNA. First, when the feline pneumonitis organism was grown in chick embryos in the presence of radioactive inorganic phosphate, both the RNA and the DNA of the purified agent had specific activities four times greater than those of the corresponding host nucleic acids.[31] Second, when thin sections of cells infected with the feline pneumonitis agent and fixed by the freeze-dry method of Gersh were treated with ribonuclease, there was a great reduction in the electron density of the agent particles.[6]

We have more recently examined the behavior of the RNA in concentrates of meningopneumonitis agent.[34–36] The content of DNA is constant, but the amount of RNA in the final concentrate varies with the mode of preparation. The highest RNA values, about twice that of the DNA, were obtained when the suspending medium was $0.08M$ ammonium acetate, in which the meningopneumonitis agent is far stabler than in any other simple salt solution. At 0 C, both nucleic acids were stable and did not leak out of the particles. At 37 C, the DNA was also stable, even after 36 hours of incubation. However, about half of the RNA appeared in the supernatant in 4 to 8 hours, after which it was lost from the particles at a much slower rate (Fig. 15), suggesting the presence of more than one macromolecular species of RNA or of more than one mechanism for its

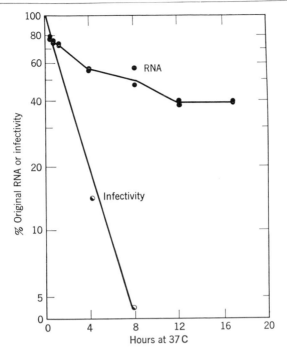

Fig. 15. Loss of RNA and infectivity from meningopneumonitis particles at 37 C. Reference 35.

degradation. The loss of RNA from meningopneumonitis particles was not accelerated by the presence of ribonuclease (Table 5). This observation supports the conclusion that the RNA lost by agent concentrates results from the intracellular breakdown of meningopneumonitis nucleic acid and not from the hydrolysis of extracellular adsorbed host RNA. Analysis of 37 C supernatants showed that the RNA appearing in the medium had been broken down to at least the level of nucleosides (Table 6).

TABLE 5

Effect of Ribonuclease on Loss of RNA from Meningopneumonitis Particles at 37 C

Measurement	Initial	After 16 Hours at 37 C	
		Without RNase	With RNase
RNA, μg P per ml	2.34	1.17	1.17
DNA, μg P per ml	1.27	1.26	1.15

Reference 36.

There is no obvious relationship between the loss of RNA and loss of infectivity, the latter declining at a much more rapid rate (Fig. 15). In other experiments, the addition of small amounts of serum albumin almost completely prevented the loss of infectivity at 37 C without having any effect on RNA breakdown, suggesting that the lost RNA is

TABLE 6

Nature of the Material Released by Meningopneumonitis Particles at 37 C

Measurement	μg P per ml
Expected from loss of RNA from particles	1.17
Found in supernatant:	
Total P	1.20
Inorganic P	1.07
260 mμ absorbancy	1.41 *
Pentose	1.06 *

* Expressed as RNA P equivalents.
Reference 36.

not vital and may be resynthesized when the depleted particle establishes itself in a new host cell. Magnesium ion, which prevents the loss of RNA from starved *Escherichia coli*,[37] did not decrease the loss of either RNA or infectivity at 37 C.

The behavior of nucleic acid in meningopneumonitis concentrates resembles that of the nucleic acids in stationary populations of bacteria (reviewed by Mandelstam [38]). The DNA is stable while the RNA is degraded to low molecular weight acid-soluble products which are released into the medium. In bacteria, RNA is stable during logarithmic growth and becomes unstable when the growth rate decreases. If this also holds true for the psittacosis group, then determination of conditions necessary for stabilization of the RNA may be one of the first steps toward the eventual extracellular cultivation of these organisms.

The occurrence of both RNA and DNA in the psittacosis group agents clearly sets them apart from the viruses which contain only one nucleic acid and never both. With the two kinds of nucleic acid present, the DNA to RNA to protein transfer of genetic information may occur just as it does in free-living cells. That it actually does occur is strongly suggested by the elegant experiments of Crocker and Eastwood.[39] From a human amnion cell line, they prepared cytoplasmic fragments which were motile, underwent pinocytosis, and incorporated amino acids but not RNA precursors. Such enucleate fragments were readily infected with a psittacosis group agent and multiplication proceeded normally. Thus growth of a psittacosis agent may occur in an enucleate fragment of a cell in which synthesis of neither DNA nor DNA-dependent RNA could have proceeded in the absence of infection. It is most logical to conclude that the agent itself provides the enzyme systems for these syntheses.

REFERENCES

1. Meyer, K. F., *Medicine*, **21**, 175 (1942).
2. Bedson, S. P., *J. Roy. Inst. Public Health Hygiene*, **22**, 67 (1959).
3. Weiss, E., *Ann. Rev. Microbiol.*, **9**, 227 (1955).
4. Wenner, H. A., *Adv. Virus Res.*, **5**, 40 (1958).
5. Litwin, J., *J. Infectious Diseases*, **101**, 100 (1957).
6. Litwin, J., *J. Infectious Diseases*, **105**, 129 (1959).
7. Litwin, J., J. E. Officer, A. Brown, and J. W. Moulder, *J. Infectious Diseases*, **109**, 251 (1961).
8. Officer, J. E., and A. Brown, *J. Infectious Diseases*, **107**, 283 (1960).
9. Higashi, N., A. Tamura, and M. Iwanaga, *Ann. N. Y. Acad. Sci.*, **98**, 100 (1962).
10. Litwin, J., *Ann. N. Y. Acad. Sci.*, **98**, 145 (1962).
11. Morgan, C., R. A. Rifkind, and H. M. Rose, *Cold Spring Harbor Symp. Quant. Biol.*, **27**, 57 (1962).
12. Allison, A. C., and K. Sandelin, *J. Exptl. Med.*, **117**, 879 (1963).
13. Gaylord, W. H., *J. Exptl. Med.*, **100**, 575 (1954).
14. Officer, J. E., and A. Brown, *Virology*, **14**, 88 (1961).
15. Colón, J. I., and J. W. Moulder, *J. Infectious Diseases*, **103**, 109 (1958).
16. Jenkin, H. M., *J. Bacteriol.*, **80**, 639 (1960).
17. Moulder, J. W., D. L. Novosel, and I. I. Tribby, *J. Bacteriol.*, **85**, 701 (1963).
18. Tamura, A., and N. Higashi, *Virology*, **20**, 596 (1963).
19. Tribby, I. I., Master's thesis, The University of Chicago, 1963.
20. Jenkin, H. M., and J. W. Moulder, unpublished results.
21. Higashi, N., *Ann. Report Inst. Virus Res. Kyoto Univ.*, **2**, 1 (1959). (Ser. B.)
22. Hosaka, Y., and Y. Nishi, *Biken's J.*, **5**, 21 (1962).
23. Erlandson, R., and E. Allen, *Bacteriol. Proc.*, p. 131 (1963).
24. Murray, R. G. E., in I. C. Gunsalus and R. Y. Stanier, Editors, *The Bacteria*, Academic Press, New York, 1960, p. 35.
25. Gogolak, F. M., and M. R. Ross, *Virology*, **1**, 474 (1955).
26. Pirsch, J. B., unpublished results.
27. Jones, A. S., and R. T. Walker, *Nature* (London), **198**, 588 (1963).
28. Wyatt, G. R., and S. S. Cohen, *Nature* (London), **170**, 846 (1952).
29. Joklik, W. K., *J. Mol. Biol.*, **5**, 265 (1962).
30. Fuerst, C. R., and G. S. Stent, *J. Gen. Physiol.*, **40**, 73 (1956).

31. Zahler, S. A., and J. W. Moulder, *J. Infectious Diseases,* **93,** 159 (1953).
32. Allison, A. C., and D. C. Burke, *J. Gen. Microbiol.,* **27,** 181 (1962).
33. Pollard, M., and T. J. Starr, *Progress in Med. Virology,* **4,** 54 (1962).
34. Rappaport, M. R., R. Curtiss, III, H. M. Jenkin, and J. W. Moulder, *Bacteriol. Proc.,* p. 112 (1960).
35. Moulder, J. W., *Ann. N. Y. Acad. Sci.,* **98,** 92 (1962).
36. Moulder, J. W., I. I. Tribby, and M. Terman, unpublished results.
37. Dagley, S., and J. Sykes, *Nature* (London), **179,** 1249 (1957).
38. Mandelstam, J., *Bacteriol. Rev.,* **24,** 289 (1960).
39. Crocker, T. T., and J. M. Eastwood, *Virology,* **19,** 23 (1963).

2

METABOLIC PROPERTIES
OF THE PSITTACOSIS GROUP

The susceptibility of agents of the psittacosis group to many chemotherapeutic agents active against bacteria [1] was one of the earliest indications of their metabolic complexity and of their kinship with bacteria. Of the more familiar antibiotics, only streptomycin, kanamycin, and ristocetin are inactive.[2] Sulfonamides, penicillin, cephalosporin, cycloserine, the tetracyclines, erythromycin, and chloramphenicol all inhibit multiplication of psittacosis group agents. These drugs are effective and specific chemotherapeutic agents because they inhibit enzymes in bacteria that have no counterpart in their vertebrate hosts.[3] If we make the reasonable assumption that the mode of action of the antibacterial drugs is the same in the psittacosis group as in bacteria, then inhibition of the multiplication of a psittacosis agent growing inside a host cell must result from inhibition of a parasite enzyme that is not present in the host cell at all. Therefore the antibacterial drugs offer unique tools for studying enzymic reactions in the psittacosis group without the complications of possible host cell participation. However, if a drug is to be truly useful, its mode of action must be known precisely. The only chemotherapeutic drugs effective against the psittacosis group and with well-defined mechanisms of action are the sulfonamides, penicillin, and cycloserine,[3] and all three have been highly useful in biochemical characterization of these microorganisms.

Sulfonamides and the Folic Acid Metabolism of the Psittacosis Group

Sulfonamides inhibit the growth of bacteria by blocking the incorporation of p-aminobenzoic acid (pAB) into folic acid,[4, 5] whose coenzyme forms are active in one-carbon transfer and are present in all cells. Most bacteria make their own folic acid and are sulfonamide-susceptible, while a few such as the lactobacilli require exogenous folic acid and are sulfonamide-resistant, as are the folic acid-requiring higher animals. All bacteria are inhibited by structural analogues of folic acid, such as aminopterin, because they prevent the formation and functioning of folic acid coenzymes. Sulfonamide inhibition is competitively reversed by pAB and noncompetitively by folic acid. Only folic acid reverses the action of its structural analogues.

The psittacosis agents are split in two groups by their reactivity toward sulfonamides, sulfadiazine being the specific drug usually employed. No other drug produces such a sharp dichotomy of response. The agents of lymphogranuloma venereum, trachoma, mouse pneumonitis, hamster pneumonitis, and a single strain of psittacosis (6BC) are sulfadiazine-sensitive; all others are fully resistant.[6] All members of the group tested so far are inhibited by folic acid analogues.[7–9] Sulfadiazine-susceptible agents quickly gain resistance during serial passage in the presence of the

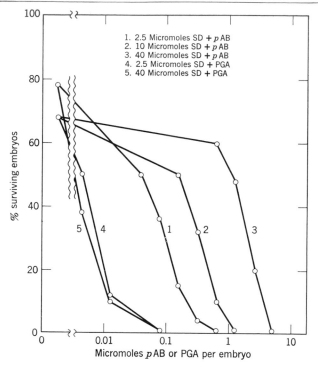

Fig. 16. Reversal of sulfadiazine inhibition of mouse pneumonitis agent multiplication by p-aminobenzoic acid and pteroylglutamic acid. Six-day-old chick embryos were inoculated via the yolk sac with 10^4 LD_{50} mouse pneumonitis agent. One hour later, sulfadiazine (SD) and pAB or pteroylglutamic acid (PGA) were given by the same route. Reference 8.

drug.[10–12] As illustrated here with the mouse pneumonitis agent growing in chick embryo yolk sac (Fig. 16),[8] pAB competitively reverses sulfadiazine inhibition of multiplication while folic acid in the form of pteroylglutamic acid acts noncompetitively in much lower concentrations.[7, 13–15] The 50 per cent reversal ratios are similar to those obtained with bacteria.[16]

Sulfadiazine prevents multiplication without immediately killing these microorganisms. Complete reversal can be obtained by giving pAB 24 hours after sulfadiazine and significant reversal is achieved even after 72 hours.[8] The susceptibility of several members of the psittacosis group to sulfadiazine is of particular importance because it indicates that, in order to multiply, these agents must synthesize folic acid from pAB, pteridine, and glutamate, a synthesis their hosts are completely incapable of carrying out.

Current concepts of the biosynthesis of folic acid in bacteria are summarized in Fig. 17. Once the dihydrofolic acid is formed, it is reduced and formylated to active coenzyme forms.[17]

Folic Acid Content of Psittacosis Group Agents. To test the hypothesis that some members of the psittacosis group make their own folic acid from simple precursors, Colón and I [18] examined agent concentrates for the presence of folic acid that could be specifically identified with the parasite and not with the host. Since the folic acid content of all living cells is exceedingly low, the usual physicochemical criteria for freedom from host contamination were inapplicable, and instead we sought evidence for the intrinsic nature of the agent folic acid which would not depend at all on the degree of purity of the concentrates analyzed. Four different agents were studied (Fig. 18). Two were sulfadiazine-resistant: feline pneumonitis and meningopneumonitis. Their folic acid must have been derived from that of the host. The other two were sulfadiazine-sensitive: mouse pneumonitis and psittacosis (strain 6BC)—and must have synthesized at least part of their own folic acid de novo. This choice of agent was made in the hope that there might be differences in the folic acid content of sulfonamide-

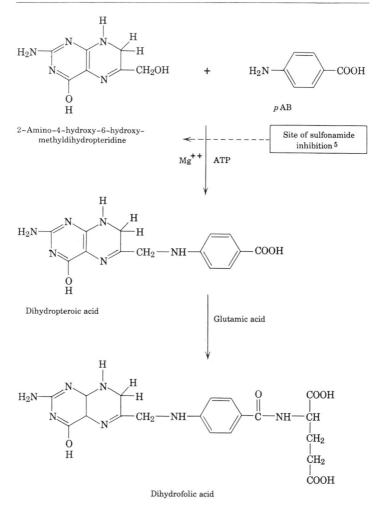

Fig. 17. Probable pathway of folic acid biosynthesis in *Escherichia coli*. Reference 95.

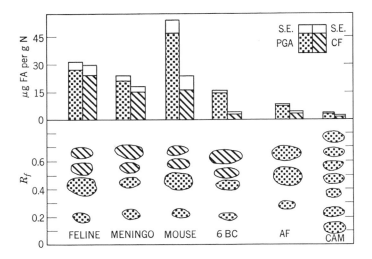

Fig. 18. Folic acid content of representative members of the psittacosis group. The agents of feline pneumonitis (FELINE), meningopneumonitis (MENINGO), mouse pneumonitis (MOUSE), and psittacosis (6BC) were concentrated from infected allantoic fluid. Their folic acid content was determined by microbiological assay (upper half of figure) and by paper chromatography-bioautography (lower half) and compared with similar determinations on uninfected allantoic fluid (AF) and chorio-allantoic membrane (CAM). The assay organisms were *Lactobacillus casei,* which responds to compounds of a complexity as great, or greater than, pteroylglutamic acid, and *Pediococcus cerevisiae,* which requires compounds with a reduced pteridine nucleus, such as leucovorin. The chromatographic solvent was isoamyl-alcohol-5% dibasic sodium phosphate, pH 9. The striped bars show the assay values with *L. casei,* while the checked bars give the results with *P. cerevisiae.* In the bio-autographs, the striped spots represent compounds active on both assay organisms; the checked spots were components active on *P. cerevisiae* alone. Six to 9 preparations of each agent were analyzed. Reference 18.

sensitive and resistant agents. All contained folic acid in amounts comparable to that found in folic acid-requiring bacteria. The average particle possessed about 100 molecules of folic acid.

Each of the four agents could be distinguished from the other three by the combined results of quantitative folic acid assay and paper chromatography-bioautography with *Lactobacillus casei* and *Pediococcus cerevisiae* as assay organisms. Only the agents of feline pneumonitis and meningopneumonitis gave identical results in the quantitative assays, and this pair was easily separated on the basis of the folic acid bioautographs. Since each agent yielded a unique folic acid analysis, it is unlikely that the agent-associated vitamin was merely adsorbed folic acid from the host, for such a conclusion would necessitate the postulation of a species-specific "nonspecific" adsorption.

By comparing R_f, relative activity for the two assay organisms, and heat stability, it was concluded that only a single major folic acid component of either infected or uninfected chick embryo fluids and tissues could have been identical with any of the four constantly occurring agent forms of folic acid. One of the major components of all four agent folic acid complexes was unique in that it was easily destroyed by heat, and no such labile compound was ever found in either uninfected or infected crude host material. These observations demonstrate that the folic acid components of agent concentrates are not the major constituents of crude tissues and fluids and that a simple concentration-dependent adsorption of host vitamin on the agent particles cannot be invoked to explain the presence of folic acid in the agent concentrates. My conclusion is that this folic acid is a specific, intrinsic part of the psittacosis agent.

In the two sulfonamide-resistant agents, the ratio of activity for *P. cerevisiae* versus the activity for *L. casei* was 0.80, while the corresponding ratio for the sensitive organisms was 0.32. This observation suggested that the hoped for analytical difference between sensitive and resistant organisms actually existed. Accordingly, the sulfonamide-resistant mutant of the 6BC strain of psittacosis derived by Golub [10] during serial egg passage with sulfadiazine was also analyzed.[8] Although it did contain considerably more folic acid than its sensitive parent, the *P. cerevisiae*/*L. casei* ratio was only 0.36. Thus, there is either no relation between folic acid content and susceptibility to sulfonamides in the psittacosis group or the basis of natural and artificially acquired resistance is not the same. Folic acid analyses for more members of the group would probably answer the question.

Folic Acid Synthesis. The demonstration of folic acid in the psittacosis group led immediately to a second hypothesis—that these organisms must have enzymes for synthesizing their own specific form of folic acid. Colón [8, 19] found that the sulfonamide-sensitive mouse pneumonitis agent forms comparatively large amounts of folic acid when incubated at 37 C (Table 7). This activity was apparent even in crude, unconcentrated infected material and was completely absent in corresponding uninfected preparations, thus emphasizing the advantage of working with parasite enzymes not represented in the host cell.

The newly synthesized folic acid, which is active for both *L. casei* and *P. cerevisiae,* is formed by two different mechanisms which may be illustrated in a single experiment (Fig. 19). When a freshly prepared concentrate of mouse pneumonitis agent was incubated at 37 C, it rapidly leaked most of its folic acid to the suspending medium. However, when such a depleted agent was reincubated, it resynthesized from endogenous sources more folic acid closely resembling in

TABLE 7

Synthesis of Folic Acid in Chick Embryo Tissues Incubated at 37 C:
Uninfected and Infected with the Agent of Mouse Pneumonitis

Folic Acid,[*] μg per g N

Preparation	Initial	After 6 hours at 37 C
Chorioallantoic membrane, crude		
Uninfected	0.2	0.2
Infected	0.2	0.4
Chorioallantoic membrane, concentrate		
Uninfected	0.0	0.0
Infected	1.0	3.1
Allantoic fluid, concentrate		
Uninfected	0.0	0.0
Infected [†]	15.6	41.2

[*] Assayed with *Pediococcus cerevisiae*.

[†] Standard concentrated preparation of mouse pneumonitis agent.

Reference 19.

chromatographic behavior and biological activity the original vitamin complement. That this was a de novo synthesis from substrates at the level of pAB was shown by the complete inhibition produced by sulfadiazine. The sulfonamide-resistant meningopneumonitis agent also exhibited an endogenous synthesis of folic acid, which occurred at a much lower rate and was not inhibited by sulfadiazine, thus furnishing an enzymic explanation for the differential drug susceptibility of the two organisms. As indicated in Fig. 17, the synthesis of folic acid is an endergonic process, requiring one mole of ATP for every mole of folic acid produced. The endogenous stores of the depleted particle are apparently sufficient to supply all necessary substrates and energy sources. This is not too surprising because the absolute amount of folic acid synthesized is very small.

The other way folic acid is formed is by the action of conjugases, enzymes that break down inactive polyglutamyl derivatives of folic acid to forms active in cell metabolism. When depleted mouse pneumonitis agent was incubated with yeast extract, there was a large increase in activity for the assay organisms. This must have been due to conjugase action because the increase was not inhibited by sulfadiazine

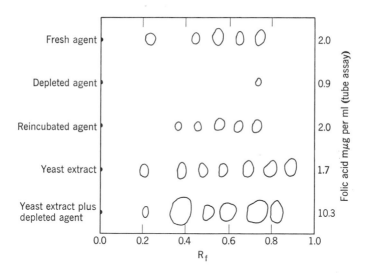

Fig. 19. Two mechanisms for folic acid formation in the agent of mouse pneumonitis. Freshly prepared concentrate was depleted of folic acid by incubation at 37 C for two hours. The washed particles were then resuspended in fresh medium and incubated 8 hours at 37 C in the presence and absence of yeast extract (Difco). The assay organism for bioautography was *L. casei,* while the tube assay was conducted with *P. cerevisiae.* Reference 19.

and did not occur when the yeast extract had first been treated with known conjugases from chick pancreas. Folic acid conjugases are also present in chick embryo tissues. However, agent conjugases and host conjugases may readily be differentiated on the basis of pH optima, cofactor requirement, and substrate specificity. The agent conjugases break down a much wider variety of conjugates than do the enzymes of the host. For example, the meningopneumonitis conjugases liberate material active for *P. cerevisiae* from a number of avian and mammalian sera and from extracts of the agent itself, while the conjugases of chorioallantoic membrane are inactive against all these sources of combined folic acid.

The interrelationships among the different forms of folic acid in a cell infected with a member of the psittacosis group is summarized in Fig. 20. I believe we have shown beyond a reasonable doubt that these microorganisms contain specific forms of folic acid and that they have enzymes capable of synthesizing it de novo and of liberating it from conjugates. The sulfonamide-sensitive members of the group

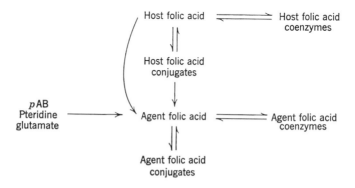

Fig. 20. Folic acid interrelationships in cells infected with psittacosis group agents.

make folic acid from pAB, pteridine, and glutamate. Like the sulfonamide-sensitive bacteria, they must carry out this synthesis, no matter how much preformed folic acid is present in their environment. Agents resistant to sulfonamides must, on the other hand, have enzymes that convert host folic acid to all their own specific forms of the vitamin. Studies with the folic acid analogue 2-deaminofolic acid support these conclusions.[8, 20] This compound inhibited the growth of *Streptococcus faecalis R* and *L. casei,* both of which are folic acid requirers, but failed to inhibit a number of microorganisms whose growth is not dependent on an exogenous source of folic acid.[21] In similar fashion, 2-deaminofolic acid inhibited multiplication of the sulfonamide-resistant feline pneumonitis agent and had no effect on the sulfonamide-sensitive mouse pneumonitis agent. 2-Deaminofolic acid was without demonstrable toxicity to chick embryos,[20] and it did not inhibit cell division in chick embryo tissue culture.[22] Therefore, it appears that the enzymes converting dietary folic acid to agent-specific forms of the vitamin are not the same as those with a similar function in the chick embryo host.

It still remains to show how folic acid functions in the metabolism of the psittacosis group. The inhibition of multiplication produced by sulfonamides and folic acid analogues shows that folic acid has a vital role in the metabolism of these organisms. As a working hypothesis, it may be assumed that at least some of the forms of folic acid made by members of the psittacosis group function as coenzymes in enzyme systems synthesizing purines, pyrimidines, amino acids, or other essential metabolites.

The Significance of Penicillin Sensitivity in the Psittacosis Group

Figure 21 is based on Strominger's [23] concept of the cyclic mechanism responsible for the synthesis of a component of

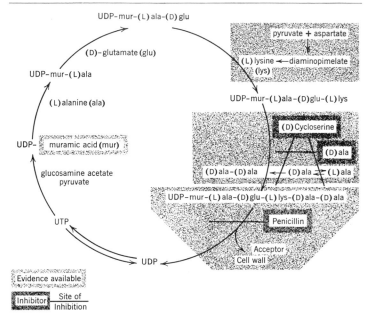

Fig. 21. Evidence for a bacterial cell wall synthesis in the psittacosis group. See text for documentation.

the cell wall of *Staphylococcus aureus*. While there is no evidence for the occurrence of precisely this series of events in the psittacosis group, the cycle nevertheless furnishes a convenient basis for discussing and interpreting the action of penicillin on these microorganisms. Also, as will become apparent in the next few pages, it is highly likely that something very similar actually does occur.

Penicillin inhibits the growth of bacteria by preventing the incorporation of a muramic acid-containing peptide into the fabric of the cell wall.[23–25] Since this mucopeptide is unique to the bacteria and the blue-green algae, it becomes clear why penicillin is chemotherapeutically effective; it inhibits a reaction in bacteria that does not occur in higher animals. Cells multiplying in the presence of penicillin produce defective walls that break up in ordinary media, and they are killed. However, in media containing nonpenetrating solutes to balance the internal osmotic pressure of the bacterial cell, new cells formed in antibiotic-containing media swell into spheroplasts, cells with nonrigid, defective walls and intact cell membranes. When penicillin is removed some spheroplasts may regain normal morphology and produce normal progeny. Others are converted into stable L-forms which produce penicillin-resistant progeny with defective cell walls and spherical shapes, even in the absence of the antibiotic.

Effect of Penicillin on Morphology. The effect of penicillin on the psittacosis group closely parallels its effect on bacteria. In varying degree, all these agents are susceptible to penicillin. Multiplication of the most sensitive ones is inhibited by levels of antibiotic effective against bacteria classified as "penicillin-sensitive." [26] Weiss [26] and Hurst et al.[27] observed that agents growing in the presence of penicillin produced large, irregularly shaped and vacuolated bodies instead of the normal particles. Tajima et al.[28] and Litwin (personal communication) saw similar structures in thin sections of penicillin-treated infected cells examined with the electron microscope (Fig. 22). Weiss [26] showed that when penicillin was removed or destroyed, these large bodies regained normal morphology, suggesting that they had remained viable during contact with penicillin. This suggestion was verified by treating infected embryos with penicillin and then injecting a potent penicillinase, which inactivated the penicillin almost instantaneously.[29] Table 8 shows that after penicillin was destroyed by penicillinase, the agent of feline pneumonitis resumed multiplication with only a

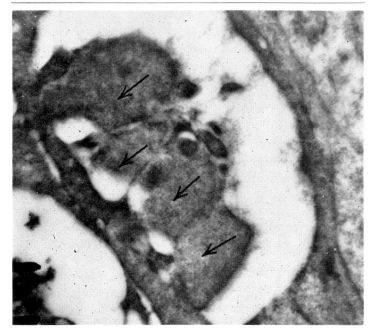

Fig. 22. Penicillin "spheroplasts" from feline pneumonitis agent. The agent grew normally in the chorioallantoic ectoderm for 20 hours. Then 100,000 units of penicillin G were given via the yolk sac, and the membranes fixed in osmium 5 hours later. Arrows indicate individual "spheroplasts" (×11,000). Reference 96.

slight lag and killed the embryos almost as quickly as if penicillin had never been present. This behavior brings to mind the observations of Eagle and Musselman [30] on the recovery from penicillin-induced bacteriostasis. These findings may be interpreted as meaning that the psittacosis group forms "spheroplasts" inside infected cells exposed to penicillin and that the cytoplasm acts as an osmotically protective medium to preserve their viability. Carey, Muschel, and Baron [31] have reached similar conclusions regarding the formation of bacterial spheroplasts in vivo. We have tried unsuccessfully to isolate the large penicillin-induced bodies by extracting infected cells with media known to preserve the integrity of bacterial spheroplasts. In vitro production of psittacosis group spheroplasts must unfortunately await in vitro cultivation.

Penicillin Resistance. Agents of the psittacosis group develop resistance to penicillin during serial yolk sac passage in the presence of the antibiotic.[32, 33] With the agent of feline pneumonitis, two distinct levels of resistance were achieved, the first after 14 passages and the second after 33.

TABLE 8

Failure of Penicillin To Kill Feline Pneumonitis Agent in vivo

Interval between Injection of Penicillin and Penicillinase (1)	Mean Survival Time of Embryos (2)	Mean Survival Time of Embryos after Penicillinase Injection (2)–(1)
No penicillinase	100% survival	
No penicillin	102 *	
0	112	112
6	122	116
24	144	120
48	173	125

* Hours.

Six-day-old chick embryos received 10^6 LD_{50} feline pneumonitis agent via the yolk sac. One thousand units of penicillin G were given in the same way immediately thereafter. Penicillinase (Bacto-Penase Concentrate, Difco) was inoculated via the yolk sac after the indicated intervals.

Reference 29.

This suggests that resistance develops step by step as it does in bacteria.[34] The fully resistant agent killed embryos given 100,000 units of penicillin, 100 times as much as required to protect to hatching embryos infected with the parent strain. In the absence of the antibiotic, both parent and resistant strains multiplied at the same rate, but in the presence of sufficient penicillin to completely stop parent growth, the resistant strain still grew at one-half the uninhibited rate (Fig. 23). Full resistance was maintained during more than 30 drugless passages.

The mechanism of resistance appears to be something other than the induction of penicillinase synthesis. First, the growth rate of the resistant feline pneumonitis agent was constant over a range of 100 to 100,000 units of penicillin per embryo, which would not be expected if the growth-limiting factor was the rate of penicillin hydrolysis. Second, the penicillin-resistant strains of both feline pneumonitis and the 6BC strain of psittacosis were just as resistant to 2,6-dimethoxyphenylpenicillin,[35] which is highly resistant to cleavage by penicillinase, as to penicillin G itself.[36]

Another type of penicillin-resistant mutant has also been obtained.[37,38] Whereas the mutants just described all multiplied at the normal parental rate in the absence of the antibiotic, this kind of resistant mutant grew only to low titer and killed embryos over a period of 5 to 10 days as compared to 1 to 2 for the strain from which they were derived. The spreading of the embryo death time led to the designation of "spread" for this mutant type. Although isolated under a variety of selective conditions, all spread mutants were completely and absolutely resistant to both penicillin and neutralizing antiserum. A number of spread mutants were isolated in the absence of penicillin by use of the growth-inhibitor 2,3-dimethylquinoxaline-1,4-N-oxide [27,39] or by neutralizing antiserum as selective agents and on one oc-

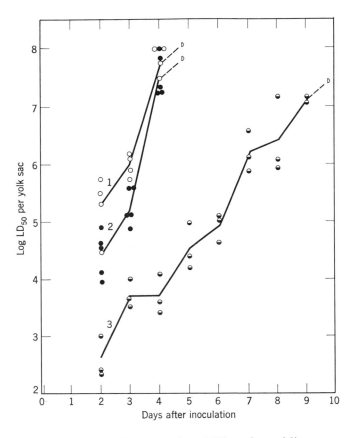

Fig. 23. Growth rates of parent and penicillin-resistant feline pneumonitis agent in the presence and absence of penicillin. 10^5 LD_{50} agent was given by the yolk sac to 6-day-old embryos and 10,000 units of penicillin by the same route one hour later. 1. Parent, no penicillin. 2. Resistant, no penicillin. 3. Resistant plus penicillin. Titer in eggs receiving parent strain and penicillin was too low to measure. Reference 32.

casion in the absence of any selection at all. The mutation to spread appears to represent a single phenotypic change, controlled by an unknown number of loci, which so alters the surface of the spread mutants as to make them unreactive toward both penicillin and neutralizing antiserum. Other evidence for the association of binding sites for both penicillin and antibody on the surface structure of the psittacosis group agents will be presented shortly. It is conceivable that the spread strains may represent defective cell wall mutants analogous to the L-forms of bacteria.[40]

Cell Walls

It had been known for some time that the organisms of the psittacosis group are contained within rigid envelopes [41] that are highly resistant to enzymes [42] and mechanical disintegration,[43] and that they are not disrupted in environments of low osmotic pressure. Therefore, the demonstration that penicillin inhibits bacterial growth by inhibiting cell wall synthesis and that its multiplication-inhibiting effects on bacteria and on the psittacosis group are strikingly similar led to the ineluctable conclusion that the psittacosis group agents must possess cell walls analogous in chemical composition and mode of biosynthesis to those of bacteria.

Jenkin [44] provided the necessary experimental confirmation by preparing cell walls from meningopneumonitis concentrates. When whole cells proved remarkably adamant to mechanical disruption, he treated them with hot deoxycholate, a reagent successfully used by Schaechter and his associates [45] in preparing rickettsial cell walls. There was a rapid loss of optical density, but electron micrographs showed no loss in electron-dense internal material. However, digestion of deoxycholate-treated cells with trypsin, an enzyme without effect on the untreated agent,[42] produced the structures shown in Fig. 24. They are rigid enough to

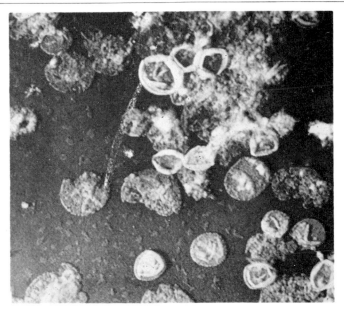

Fig. 24. Meningopneumonitis cell walls. Air-dried and chromium-shadowed (×12,500). Reference 44.

determine the size and shape of the intact cells from which they were derived, and they contain little or no electron-dense internal material. Their resemblance to bacterial cell walls is striking, and I shall call them meningopneumonitis cell walls. However, as viewed by thin section electron microscopy (Fig. 2), they do not have the thickness and complexity characteristic of bacterial cell walls. It is, therefore, possible that the cell walls of the psittacosis group may have been modified and simplified during adaptation to intracellular life.

The cell walls derived from both large and small particle types are readily discernible. In forming cell walls, the

TABLE 9

Comparison of the Chemical Composition of Meningopneumonitis
Whole Cells and Cell Walls

Measurement	Whole Cells	Cell Walls
Dry weight, *g per particle*	1.9×10^{-14}	0.9×10^{-14}
Amino acids, *number identified*	14	9
% dry weight		
Protein	33	32
Carbohydrate	2.3	1.6
Muramic acid	present	present
Total nucleic acid	5.6	<0.4
Phospholipid	7.5	1.5

Reference 44.

small particles lose their dense centers and collapse into structures strongly resembling discarded grape skins. The flat particles become even flatter, lose their electron-dense granules, and acquire a rougher surface texture. These visible surface differences are paralleled by difference in the surface charge of the two kinds of intact particles as revealed by starch electrophoresis or cellulose anion chromatography.[46]

In chemical composition, meningopneumonitis cell walls resemble those of rickettsiae[45] and Gram-negative bacteria.[24, 25] They contain practically no nucleic acid, small amounts of carbohydrate, large amounts of lipid, and a variety of amino acids (Table 9). Lysine is present and diaminopimelic acid is absent.

Muramic Acid. The presence or absence of muramic acid (Fig. 25) in an organism is of peculiar taxonomic significance because this amino sugar has been found only in bacteria.[24, 25] Furthermore, all bacteria investigated so far have a muramic acid-containing mucopeptide as a part of their cell walls. Muramic acid appears to function by linking peptides through an amide bond at its carboxyl group to other sugars via a glycosidic link at its terminal hydroxyl group.

The presence of muramic acid in whole cells and cell walls of meningopneumonitis [44] and whole cells of mouse pneumonitis [47] was reported almost simultaneously. More recently, Perkins and Allison [48] have positively identified muramic in four members of the psittacosis group, the agents of psittacosis, trachoma, feline pneumonitis, and mouse pneumonitis. They used two rigorous criteria. First, the suspected muramic acid was converted to its N-acetyl derivative with C^{14}-labeled acetic anhydride and its identity with authentic N-acetyl-muramic acid established by chromatography. Second, muramic acid is known to be converted to 2-O-carboxyethylarabinose by ninhydrin. Therefore, samples of the suspected muramic acid were treated with ninhydrin and the reaction product identified as 2-O-carboxyethylarabinose by chromatographic comparison with an authentic sample. These results firmly establish the

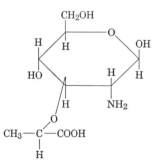

Fig. 25. Muramic acid (3-O-carboxyethyl-D-glucosamine).

presence of muramic acid in members of the psittacosis group, and it may reasonably be assumed that its function is as in bacteria (Fig. 21). It may also be assumed that agents of the psittacosis group contain enzymes for its synthesis, but so far this hypothesis has not been tested.

Serologic Properties of Cell Walls. Much of the serologic reactivity of bacteria resides in their cell walls and this is also true for the psittacosis group.[49, 50] All of the important antigens of the psittacosis group were found in meningopneumonitis cell walls, with the exception of the group-specific complement-fixing antigen (Table 10). It appeared unchanged in the deoxycholate extract and well may have been extracted from the cell walls.

Members of the psittacosis group contain a particle-associated, unstable toxin which kills mice a few hours after

TABLE 10

Comparison of the Serologic Properties of Meningopneumonitis Whole Cells and Cell Walls

	Antigen Present in		
Serologic Test	Whole Cells	Cell Walls	Deoxy-cholate Extract
Infectivity neutralization *	+	+	0
Toxin neutralization *	+	+	0
Direct and indirect complement fixation			
Group-specific	+	0	+
Species-specific	− †	+	0

* Measured by specific absorption of neutralizing antibodies.
† Obscured by group-specific antigen.
References 49, 50.

intravenous injection and is neutralized by fowl antiserum with a high degree of species specificity.[51, 52] The infectivity of these agents is also neutralized with the same high specificity by fowl antiserum.[53, 54] Both neutralizing activities are specifically removed from antiserum by absorption with meningopneumonitis cell walls, although the walls are neither infective nor toxic. Cell walls also enter into a complement fixation reaction of specificity equal to that of toxin and infectivity neutralization. This suggests that all three specific serologic activities reside in a single cell wall antigen, but more work is needed for actual proof.

Since penicillin acts by interfering with cell wall synthesis and since the antigen responsible for neutralization of infectivity by antiserum is located in the cell wall, it is not surprising that the spread mutants previously discussed become simultaneously resistant to both penicillin and antiserum.

The presence of stable, species-specific complement-fixing antigens in psittacosis group cell walls offers the possibility of a useful new tool in the practical serology of the psittacosis group. Jenkin (personal communication) has successfully differentiated four different agents in this manner.

Amino Acid Metabolism

D-Cycloserine and D-Alanine. The antibiotic D-cycloserine (Fig. 26) offers another probe for searching out enzymes in the psittacosis group. The first clue to its mode of action came from the finding that the growth-inhibiting effects of the antibiotic are competitively reversed by its structural analogue D-alanine (Fig. 26).[55–58] This relationship was explained by Strominger, Ito, and Threnn,[59] who demonstrated that D-cycloserine inhibits both the alanine racemase and the D-alanyl-D-alanine synthetase of *Staphylococcus aureus* and that D-alanine competitively reverses both inhibitions (Fig. 21). Neuhaus and Lynch [60] have reported similar findings on the D-alanyl-D-alanine synthetase of *Streptococcus faecalis*. Since the D-alanine dipeptide is a portion of the cell wall mucopeptide (Fig. 19), these results explain the inhibition of cell wall synthesis by D-cycloserine first observed by Ciak and Hahn.[61]

Because the psittacosis group has cell walls like bacteria, it could be predicted that D-cycloserine would inhibit their growth and that D-alanine would relieve the inhibition. When the agents of psittacosis (6BC), meningopneumonitis, feline pneumonitis, and mouse pneumonitis were grown in the chick embryo yolk sac, they were all inhibited by D-cycloserine and the inhibition was reversed by D-alanine.[62] The agent of mouse pneumonitis was exceptionally sensitive to the antibiotic (Fig. 27). D-Alanine competitively reversed the growth-inhibiting action of D-cycloserine on this agent over a range of 5 to 100 micromoles antibiotic per embryo. This range of inhibitor concentration was limited at one extreme by the toxicity of the antibiotic and at the other by the susceptibility of the mouse pneumonitis agent. A ratio of 2 moles of D-alanine to 1 of D-cycloserine gave half-maximal inhibition, a value comparable to that obtained in bacteria.

Of a number of compounds structurally related to D-ala-

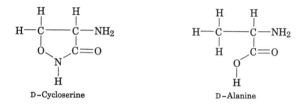

Fig. 26. D-Cycloserine (D-4-amino-3-isoxazolidone) and D-alanine.

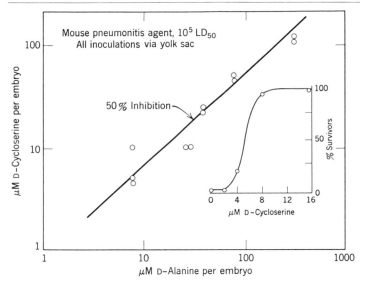

Fig. 27. Inhibition of the multiplication of the agent of mouse pneumonitis by D-cycloserine and its competitive reversal by D-alanine.

nine, only DL-alanyl-DL-alanine reversed the D-cycloserine inhibition of mouse pneumonitis agent multiplication. Since, mole for mole, the racemic dipeptide was just as effective as D-alanine, it seems likely that it acts by being hydrolyzed to free alanine, presumably by a mouse pneumonitis dipeptidase. Mixtures of pyruvate and D-aspartate or D-glutamate were inactive as reversers of the D-cycloserine inhibition, suggesting the absence of a D-amino acid transaminase [63] in the mouse pneumonitis agent.

In the presence of D-cycloserine, the mouse pneumonitis agent appeared in large, dense and swollen forms strikingly similar to those seen when the agent grew in the presence of penicillin (Fig. 28). In analogy with the penicillin-pro-

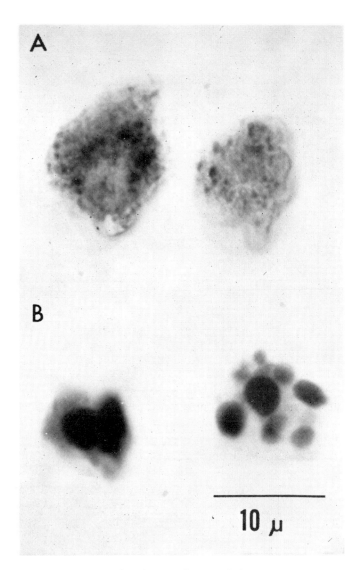

Fig. 28. Effect of D-cycloserine on the morphology of mouse pneumonitis agent growing in the chorioallantoic ectoderm of the chick embryo. (A) Untreated, fixed and stained 40 hours after infection. (B) Treated with 20 micromoles of D-cycloserine 16 hours after infection, fixed and stained 24 hours thereafter with Giemsa stain (×3000). Reference 62.

duced abnormal forms, they may be considered as spheroplasts produced in vivo by the interference in cell wall
synthesis by D-cycloserine. Injection of D-alanine into
D-cycloserine-inhibited embryos effectively restored multiplication of the agent of mouse pneumonitis when the in-
terval between injection of inhibitor and antagonist was
prolonged for as long as 72 hours. This shows that D-cyclo-
serine-induced spheroplasts resume multiplication when the
action of the antibiotic is antagonized by D-alanine.

Inhibition of the multiplication of members of the psittacosis group by D-cycloserine and its specific reversal by
D-alanine is good evidence of the existence of a D-cycloserine-sensitive, D-alanine-requiring enzymic reaction that is
vital to the reproduction of these microorganisms. It is
highly likely that the inhibited reaction is alanine racemase,
D-alanyl-D-alanine synthetase, or both. These two enzymes
are peculiar to the metabolism of bacteria, and it is almost
certain that the D-cycloserine-sensitive enzyme is synthesized
by the psittacosis group agents and not by their hosts. Since
the major function of D-alanine in bacteria is incorporation
into the cell wall mucopeptide in the form of its dipeptide,
these experiments offer further evidence for the homology
of bacterial and psittacosis group cell walls.

Diaminopimelic Acid Decarboxylase. Bacterial cell wall
mucopeptides contain either lysine or its immediate pre-
cursor diaminopimelic acid (DAP), and sometimes both.[25]
As already mentioned, meningopneumonitis cell walls have
lysine and no DAP. Bader and Morgan [64] observed that
lysine is not required for multiplication of the 6BC strain
of psittacosis in L cells, although it is a constituent of the
agent [65] and is required for growth of the L cells themselves.[66] This suggested that the psittacosis group agents
may synthesize their own lysine via DAP as do bacteria
(Fig. 21).[67, 68]

The hypothesis was put to test by examining meningopneumonitis concentrates for DAP decarboxylase, the enzyme catalyzing the final reaction in the bacterial synthesis of lysine (Fig. 29).[69] Again the search was facilitated by the absence of this enzyme in the chick embryo host. Meningopneumonitis concentrates were incubated at 37 C and lysine production was followed by paper chromatography-bioautography and microbiological assay with a lysine-requiring mutant of *Escherichia coli*.[70] In the absence of any additions, there was a small accumulation of lysine and several other amino acids (Table 11). When DAP was added there was a two- to fivefold increase in lysine synthesis which was further increased by the simultaneous addition of pyridoxal phosphate. There was no lysine accumulation during incubation of fresh concentrates at 0 C or of boiled ones at 37 C, either with or without added DAP. The activity of DAP decarboxylase in the meningopneumonitis agent is about the same as in the weakly active bacteria studied by Dewey.[71] Active cell-free extracts were readily prepared from sonically disrupted particles. Since these particles had

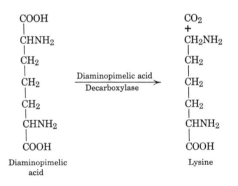

Fig. 29. Diaminopimelic acid and lysine.

TABLE 11

Diaminopimelic Acid Decarboxylase in Meningopneumonitis Agent

	Lysine Produced in 18 Hours at 37 C μM/mg protein	
Additions	Intact Cells *	Sonic Extract †
None	26	165
DAP, $5 \times 10^{-3}M$	59	496
DAP, $5 \times 10^{-3}M$ and pyridoxal phosphate, $10^{-4}M$	80	596

* Mean of 7 experiments.
† Mean of 3 experiments.
Reference 70.

never been in contact with exogenous DAP, the preparation of active extracts shows that the meningopneumonitis DAP decarboxylase is constitutive, as it is in bacteria. It also resembles the bacterial enzyme in its pH optimum and Michaelis-Menton constant.[69]

In bacteria, DAP decarboxylase is specific for the *meso*-enantiomorph of the amino acid, and a DAP racemase interconverting the L*- and *meso*-forms is present.[72] The D-isomer is metabolically inert. Whole cells and cell-free extracts of the meningopneumonitis agent decarboxylated the L- and *meso*-isomers of DAP but not the D-.[36] Since the L-enantiomorph was decarboxylated more slowly than the *meso*-form, the meningopneumonitis agent probably also contains a DAP racemase.

The principal, and probably only, pathway of lysine syn-

* The enantiomorphic forms of DAP were kindly supplied by Dr. Lionel E. Rhuland of The Upjohn Company, Kalamazoo, Michigan.

thesis in bacteria is via DAP.[73] Therefore, the presence of
DAP decarboxylase in the meningopneumonitis agent and
the absence of an exogenous lysine requirement for growth
of the psittacosis agent in L cells may be explained by
assuming that the members of the psittacosis group can
make their own lysine by way of DAP from starting mate-
rials such as pyruvate and asparate. We are now attempting
to show DAP synthesis in the meningopneumonitis agent,
but have not yet obtained clear-cut positive results. Lower
fungi, green algae, and higher plants also employ the DAP
pathway for lysine biosynthesis.[74–76] However, it seems unlikely that any of these organisms are the evolutionary
forebears of the psittacosis group, and the existence of an
enzyme active against DAP is further evidence for the bacterial ancestry of these microorganisms.

Breakdown of Agent Protein in vitro. As mentioned
in the previous section, when meningopneumonitis concentrates were incubated at 37 C in the absence of added
substrates or cofactors, a number of ninhydrin-positive substances appeared in the supernatant. More detailed investigation of this phenomenon disclosed a protein breakdown
of unexpected magnitude.[77] The release of ninhydrin re-
active substances from meningopneumonitis whole particles
held at 37 C was followed by two-dimensional paper chromatography and by the quantitative ninhydrin reaction.
Both amino acids and small peptides were released at slowly
decreasing rates for 18 to 24 hours until as much as one-fifth
of the agent protein was broken down. When 37 C supernatants were hydrolyzed with acid, their two-dimensional
chromatograms were indistinguishable from those of comparable chromatograms of acid-hydrolyzed whole particles,
indicating that the protein broken down at 37 C was not a
special fraction but was representative of the agent protein
as a whole.

There was no hydrolysis of protein in fresh concentrates held at 0 C or in boiled concentrates held at 37 C. Preparations of washed particles from uninfected chorioallantoic membrane did not liberate amino acids or peptides at 37 C. It thus appears that the meningopneumonitis agent contains a proteinase that becomes active when the agent particles are incubated in vitro at 37 C and that this enzyme then hydrolyzes large amounts of the agent protein and releases it into the suspending medium as amino acids and peptides. It is not known whether or not this proteinase is involved in the breakdown of host cytoplasm.

The findings furnish an explanation for the slow accumulation of lysine in the absence of DAP noted in previous experiments (Table 10). However, they have much more important implications. It is obvious that this high level of proteinase activity must seriously interfere with the attempts to demonstrate in vitro enzymic activity in the meningopneumonitis agent. It is also equally obvious that one of the first steps toward the eventual extracellular cultivation of members of the psittacosis group must be the finding of conditions under which their proteins can be stabilized at growth temperatures outside host cells.

Action of the Tetracyclines on the Psittacosis Group

It is unfortunate that so little is known about the mode of action of the tetracyclines,[3] because of all common chemotherapeutic agents they are the most active against the psittacosis group [1, 6, 78] and have almost completely supplanted other forms of therapy. However, we have obtained some results with a chlortetracycline-resistant mutant of mouse pneumonitis agent which, to reverse the tables for once, may possibly be of value in the eventual elucidation of the mode of action of the drug.

The chlortetracycline-resistant mutant was obtained by

Greenland and Moulder [79] by 5 serial yolk sac passages in minimal inhibitory amounts of the antibiotic. It quickly kills embryos given several times the amount of chlortetracycline needed to protect completely embryos infected with the parent agent and is stable indefinitely during drugless

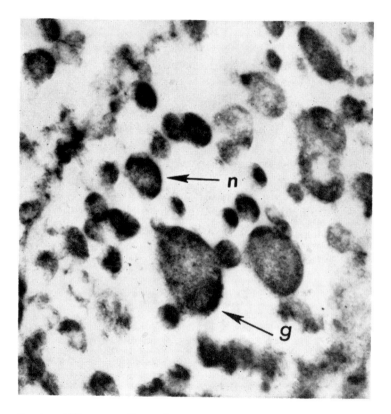

Fig. 30. Chlortetracycline-resistant mouse pneumonitis agent in the chorioallantoic ectoderm 30 hours after infection. Osmium-fixed (×12,000). n = normal particle. g = giant particle. Reference: Litwin, unpublished.

passage. The resistant mutant also has a number of new properties not directly connected with the ability to multiply in the presence of the antibiotic. It has a 72-hour growth cycle instead of the normal 30-hour one, and it produces in the complete absence of any inhibitor far more very large particles than any other psittacosis group agent so far examined (Fig. 30).[79, 80] The dose of D-cycloserine required to reduce chick embryo mortality to 50 per cent is 10 times greater than that required for the parent strain (see Fig. 25), and antiserum against the mutant does not neutralize the parent and vice versa.[81]

The lengthened growth cycle and the presence of many exceptionally large particles is indicative of a disturbance in multiplication, particularly in division mechanisms, while the increased resistance to D-cycloserine and the changes in specificity of the neutralizing antigen most probably reflect a change in the particle surface. One may, therefore, speculate that in the mouse pneumonitis agent chlortetracycline inhibits, directly or indirectly, the synthesis or functioning of some vital component of the cell wall or membrane, that the resistant mutant can multiply in the presence of the antibiotic because it contains an altered surface component, and that this alteration is responsible for the other changes in agent properties concomitant to the development of resistance to chlortetracycline.

Nutritional Requirements for Multiplication of the Psittacosis Group

Bader and Morgan [64, 82] studied the requirements for the reproduction of the sulfonamide-sensitive 6BC strain of psittacosis in cultures of L cells whose nutritional requirements had already been worked out in detail by Eagle.[66, 83] If the L cells were kept in a balanced salts-glucose medium for two days prior to infection, the psittacosis agent infected the depleted cells but was unable to multiply. If enriched medium was added at any time up to 4 days after infection, the psittacosis agent began to multiply at a normal rate. This furnished a sensitive system for studying nutritional requirements for growth of the psittacosis group. A synthetic medium containing amino acids, B-vitamins, glucose, and inorganic salts proved capable of initiating propagation of the psittacosis agent in the depleted L cells. Systematic variation in the individual components of the medium then allowed establishment of minimum requirements for psittacosis growth in L cells. No amino acid not required for L cell growth was essential for psittacosis multiplication. However, four amino acids and two vitamins necessary for L cell growth were not required by the psittacosis agent: arginine, histidine, lysine, glutamine, folic acid, and riboflavin. Of the four, arginine and histidine are completely or almost completely absent from agent proteins, thus explaining their dispensability. However, lysine is present in relatively large amounts. Here, the requirement seems to be met by the synthesis of DAP from pyruvate and asparate and its subsequent decarboxylation to lysine. The lack of a glutamine requirement is hard to assess. It functions in many metabolic reactions, frequently more as a coenzyme than as a substrate for protein synthesis. Perhaps the psittacosis group can synthesize glutamine from glutamate, ammonia, and ATP.[84] The absence of a folic acid requirement is easily explained by the ability of the 6BC strain of psittacosis to make this vitamin. The dispensability of riboflavin is very interesting because cytochrome c reductase is a flavoprotein and Allen and Bovarnick [85, 86] have demonstrated cytochrome c reductase activity in the group. Thus, it is now possible to give a reasonably plausible explanation of the nutritional requirements for multiplication of the psittacosis group in terms of their known biochemical properties.

Experimental Simulation of the Latent State

An outstanding characteristic of natural infections with members of the psittacosis group is the frequency with which latent infections are encountered. These microorganisms may persist for long periods in the tissues of man,[87] mice,[88, 89] and chick embryos [90, 91] without harm to their hosts. Many other psittacosis group infections probably also exhibit latent phases.

Although complete explanation of the mechanisms of latency in infections with these organisms is still lacking, three different kinds of laboratory experiments bear directly on the problem. Table 12 summarizes a number of observations showing that active multiplication of a psittacosis group agent may be interrupted for several days by one experimental manipulation and reinitiated by a second. Such a phenomenon is in a real sense an experimental simulation of the natural latent state.

The first group of experimental latencies were all produced by the action of an inhibitor of agent multiplication and interrupted by destruction or antagonism of the inhibitor. These observations demonstrate that a nonmultiplying organism is not necessarily destroyed by the host cell in which it is lodged and that it may remain there for some time in a potentially viable state. Penicillin, sulfadiazine, and D-cycloserine all specifically inhibit enzymic reactions without counterpart in the vertebrate host, but aminopterin, which can induce an exceptionally long period of experimental latency,[9] is a potent inhibitor of metabolic processes in both host and parasite, and its effects may well be a combination of direct action on the agent and starvation of the host as described in the next paragraph.

In the second type of experimental latency, tissue culture cells were starved by incubation in simple salts-glucose solu-

TABLE 12

Experimental Simulation of the Latent State

Agent	Host	Latency Induced by	Normal Multiplication Restored by	Duration of Latency, Days	Reference
Feline pneumonitis	Chick embryo	Penicillin	Penicillinase	3 *	29
Mouse pneumonitis	Chick embryo	Sulfadiazine	p-Aminobenzoate	3 *	8
Mouse pneumonitis	Chick embryo	D-Cycloserine	D-Alanine	3 *	62
Psittacosis (TT)	McCoy cells	Aminopterin	Leucovorin	28	9
Psittacosis (6BC)	Chick embryo cells †	Salts-glucose solution	Complete growth medium	15	92
Psittacosis (6BC)	L cells	Salts-glucose solution	Complete growth medium	3	93
Feline pneumonitis	Chick embryo	Early passage	Incubation prolonged	Indefinite	94

* Longest time tested. † Primary culture.

tion and then infected with a psittacosis group agent. Invasion proceeded normally, the infection was established, but active multiplication did not begin until the salt solution had been replaced by a complete growth medium for cells being used. Morgan and Bader [92, 93] have suggested that latency may result from nutritional deficiencies in host cells and that recrudescence of active infection may result when the deficiencies are corrected. The nutritional deficiencies encountered in nature would be much less severe than those produced by incubating tissue culture cells in inorganic salt solutions, but it is entirely possible that the intracellular concentration of a metabolite essential for psittacosis group multiplication might fall below a critical level under one set of conditions and then arise above it under another, all in a generally well-nourished host.

The third method for simulating latency in the laboratory is to subject a psittacosis agent to very rapid serial passage. Thus, Litwin [94] infected the chorioallantoic ectoderm of the chick embryo with the feline pneumonitis agent, and repassed it in the same manner 15 hours after infection. The growth cycle was greatly delayed, and small particles capable of initiating a normal cycle did not appear for 90 hours. If this delayed cycle was terminated by passage at 50 hours, the cycle was again delayed and fully infectious particles did not appear. In this manner, the feline pneumonitis agent was indefinitely transferred from one embryo to the other without the appearance of normal infectious particles, but normal progeny were always produced after prolonged incubation either on the chorioallantoic ectoderm or in yolk sac.

A plausible general explanation for all three types of experimental latency is that the latency-inducing factor, be it inhibitor, starvation, or rapid passage, interferes in some manner with the reorganization of the invading particle into the vegetative multiplying form (see Chapter 1). In other words, the first stage in the growth cycle normally taking about 10 hours is indefinitely prolonged. This hypothesis is by no means proven, but it offers a basis for further experimentation. Whether this idea proves right or wrong, it is encouraging that the problem of latency in the psittacosis group may now be approached in terms of concepts gained from biochemical study of its multiplication.

REFERENCES

1. Hurst, E. W., *Brit. Med. Bull.*, **9**, 180 (1953).
2. Gordon, F. B., and A. L. Quan, *Ann. N. Y. Acad. Sci.*, **98**, 261 (1962).
3. Davis, B. D., and D. S. Feingold, in I. C. Gunsalus, and R. Y. Stanier, Editors, *The Bacteria*, Academic Press, New York, 1962, Vol. 4, p. 343.
4. Woods, D. D., *Brit. J. Exptl. Pathol.*, **21**, 74 (1940).
5. Brown, G. M., *J. Biol. Chem.*, **237**, 536 (1962).
6. Wenner, H. A., *Adv. Virus Res.*, **5**, 40 (1958).
7. Morgan, H. R., *J. Exptl. Med.*, **88**, 285 (1948).
8. Colón, J. I., *Ann. N. Y. Acad. Sci.*, **98**, 234 (1962).
9. Pollard, M., and N. Sharon, *Proc. Soc. Exptl. Biol. Med.*, **112**, 51 (1963).
10. Golub, O. J., *J. Lab. Clin. Med.*, **33**, 1241 (1948).
11. Loosli, C. G., D. Hamre, J. T. Grayston, and E. R. Alexander, *Antibiotics Ann.*, p. 490 (1954–1955).
12. Johnston, P. B., J. T. Grayston, and P. C. Chen, *Ann. N. Y. Acad. Sci.*, **98**, 283 (1962).
13. Findlay, G. M., *Brit. J. Exptl. Pathol.*, **21**, 356 (1940).
14. Morgan, H. R., *J. Exptl. Med.*, **95**, 269 (1952).
15. Huang, J., and M. D. Eaton, *J. Bacteriol.*, **58**, 73 (1949).
16. Fox, C. L., and H. M. Rose, *Proc. Soc. Exptl. Biol. Med.*, **50**, 142 (1942).
17. Huennekins, F. M., and M. J. Osborn, *Adv. Enzymol.*, **21**, 369 (1959).
18. Colón, J. I., and J. W. Moulder, *J. Infectious Diseases*, **103**, 109 (1958).
19. Colón, J. I., *J. Bacteriol.*, **79**, 741 (1960).
20. Colón, J. I., Doctoral dissertation, The University of Chicago, 1959.

21. Nimmo-Smith, R. H., and D. J. Brown, *J. Gen. Microbiol.*, **9**, 536 (1953).

22. Brown, D. J., *J. Chem. Soc.*, **1953**, 1644.

23. Strominger, J. L., *Fed. Proc.*, **21**, 134 (1962).

24. Salton, M. J., *Microbial Cell Walls*, John Wiley & Sons, New York, 1960.

25. Perkins, H. R., *Bacteriol. Rev.*, **27**, 18 (1963).

26. Weiss, E., *J. Infectious Diseases*, **87**, 249 (1950).

27. Hurst, E. W., J. K. Landquist, P. Melvin, J. M. Peters, N. Senior, J. A. Silk, and G. J. Stacey, *Brit. J. Pharm. Chemotherapy*, **8**, 297 (1953).

28. Tajima, M., T. Samejima, and Y. Nomura, *J. Bacteriol.*, **77**, 23 (1959).

29. Moulder, J. W., J. I. Colón, J. Ruda, and M. M. Zebovitz, *J. Infectious Diseases*, **98**, 229 (1956).

30. Eagle, H., and A. D. Musselman, *J. Bacteriol.*, **58**, 475 (1949).

31. Carey, W. F., L. H. Muschel, and L. S. Baron, *J. Immunol.*, **84**, 183 (1960).

32. Moulder, J. W., B. R. S. McCormak, F. M. Gogolak, M. M. Zebovitz, and M. K. Itatani, *J. Infectious Diseases*, **96**, 57 (1955).

33. Gordon, F. B., V. W. Andrew, and J. C. Wagner, *Virology*, **4**, 156 (1957).

34. Demerec, M., *J. Bacteriol.*, **56**, 63 (1948).

35. Knight, V., P. A. Bunn, H. G. Steinman, and P. Fireman, *Antibiotics Chemotherapy*, **9**, 537 (1961).

36. Novosel, D. M., and J. W. Moulder, unpublished results.

37. Moulder, J. W., J. Ruda, J. I. Colón, and R. M. Greenland, *J. Infectious Diseases*, **102**, 186, 1958.

38. Woodroofe, G. M., and J. W. Moulder, *J. Infectious Diseases*, **107**, 195 (1960).

39. Greenland, R. M., and J. W. Moulder, *J. Infectious Diseases*, **102**, 294 (1958).

40. Lederberg, J., and J. St. Clair, *J. Bacteriol.*, **75**, 143 (1958).

41. Hamre, D., H. Rake, and G. Rake, *J. Exptl. Med.*, **86**, 1 (1947).

42. Brown, A., M. K. Itatani, and J. W. Moulder, *J. Infectious Diseases*, **91**, 184 (1952).

43. Ross, M. R., and F. M. Gogolak, *Virology*, **3**, 343 (1957).

44. Jenkin, H. M., *J. Bacteriol.*, **80**, 639 (1960).

45. Schaechter, M., A. J. Tousmis, Z. A. Cohn, H. Rosen, J. Campbell, and F. E. Hahn, *J. Bacteriol.*, **74**, 822 (1957).

46. Jenkin, H. M., and J. W. Moulder, unpublished results.

47. Allison, A. C., and H. R. Perkins, *Nature*, **188**, 796 (1960).

48. Perkins, H. R., and A. C. Allison, *J. Gen. Microbiol.*, **30**, 469 (1963).

49. Jenkin, H. M., M. R. Ross, and J. W. Moulder, *J. Immunol.*, **86**, 123 (1961).

50. Ross, M. R., and H. M. Jenkin, *Ann. N. Y. Acad. Sci.*, **98**, 329 (1962).

51. Rake, G., and H. P. Jones, *J. Exptl. Med.*, **79**, 463 (1944).

52. Manire, G. P., and K. F. Meyer, *J. Infectious Diseases*, **86**, 241 (1950).

53. Hilleman, M. R., *J. Infectious Diseases*, **76**, 96 (1945).

54. St. John, E., and F. B. Gordon, *J. Infectious Diseases*, **80**, 297 (1947).

55. Bondi, A., J. Kornblum, and C. Forte, *Proc. Soc. Exptl. Biol. Med.*, **96**, 270 (1957).

56. Shockman, G. D., *Proc. Soc. Exptl. Biol. Med.*, **101**, 693 (1959).

57. Morrison, N. E., *Bacteriol. Proc.*, p. 86 (1962).

58. Zygmunt, W. A., *J. Bacteriol.*, **84**, 154 (1962).

59. Strominger, J. L., E. Ito, and R. H. Threnn, *J. Am. Chem. Soc.*, **82**, 998 (1960.)

60. Neuhaus, F. C., and J. L. Lynch, *Biochem. Biophys. Res. Comm.*, **8**, 377 (1962).

61. Ciak, J., and F. E. Hahn, *Antibiotics Chemotherapy*, **9**, 47 (1959).

62. Moulder, J. W., D. L. Novosel, and J. E. Officer, *J. Bacteriol.*, **85**, 707 (1963).

63. Thorne, C. B., C. G. Gomez, and R. D. Housewright, *J. Bacteriol.*, **69**, 357 (1955).

64. Bader, J. P., and H. R. Morgan, *J. Exptl. Med.*, **108**, 617 (1958).

65. Ross, M. R., and F. M. Gogolak, *Virology*, **3**, 365 (1957)

66. Eagle, H., *J. Biol. Chem.*, **214**, 839 (1955).

67. Dewey, D. L., and E. Work, *Nature*, **169**, 533 (1952).

68. Davis, B. D., *Nature*, **169**, 534 (1952).

69. Dewey, D. L., D. S. Hoare, and E. Work, *Biochem. J.*, **58**, 523 (1954).

70. Moulder, J. W., D. L. Novosel, and I. I. Tribby, *J. Bacteriol.*, **85**, 701 (1963).

71. Dewey, D. L., *J. Gen. Microbiol.*, **11**, 307 (1954).

72. Hoare, D. S., and E. Work, *Biochem. J.*, **61**, 562 (1955).

73. Rhuland, L. E., and R. D. Hamilton, *Biochim. Biophys. Acta.*, **51**, 525 (1961).

74. Vogel, H. J., *Proc. Natl. Acad. Sci. U. S.*, **45**, 1717 (1959).

75. Vogel, H. J., *Biochim. Biophys. Acta.*, **34**, 282 (1959).

76. Vogel, H. J., *Biochim. Biophys. Acta.*, **41**, 172 (1960).

77. Moo-Penn, G. L., Master's thesis, The University of Chicago, 1963.

78. Weiss, E., *Ann. Rev. Microbiol.*, **9**, 227 (1955).
79. Greenland, R. M., and J. W. Moulder, *J. Infectious Diseases*, **108**, 293 (1961).
80. Litwin, J., J. E. Officer, A. Brown, and J. W. Moulder, *J. Infectious Diseases*, **109**, 251 (1961).
81. Moulder, J. W., D. L. Novosel, and I. I. Tribby, unpublished results.
82. Bader, J. P., and H. R. Morgan, *J. Exptl. Med.*, **113**, 271 (1961).
83. Eagle, H., *J. Exptl. Med.*, **102**, 595 (1955).
84. Meister, A., in P. D. Boyer, H. Lardy, and K. Myrback, Editors, *The Enzymes*, Ed. 2, Academic Press, New York, 1962, Vol. VI, p. 443.
85. Allen, E. G., and M. R. Bovarnick, *J. Exptl. Med.*, **105**, 539 (1957).
86. Allen, E. G., and M. R. Bovarnick, *Ann. N. Y. Acad. Sci.*, **98**, 229 (1962).
87. Meyer, K. F., and B. Eddie, *J. Infectious Diseases*, **88**, 109 (1951).
88. Bedson, S. P., *Brit. J. Exptl. Pathol.*, **19**, 353 (1938).
89. Early, R. L., and H. R. Morgan, *J. Immunol.*, **53**, 251 (1946).
90. Davis, D. J., and J. E. Vogel, *Proc. Soc. Exptl. Biol. Med.*, **70**, 585 (1949).
91. Greenland, R. M., *J. Infectious Diseases*, **108**, 287 (1961).
92. Morgan, H. R., *J. Exptl. Med.*, **103**, 37 (1956).
93. Morgan, H. R., and J. C. Bader, *J. Exptl. Med.*, **106**, 39 (1957).
94. Litwin, J., *J. Infectious Diseases*, **105**, 129 (1959).
95. Brown, G. M., R. A. Weisman, and D. M. Molnar, *J. Biol. Chem.*, **236**, 2534 (1961).
96. Moulder, J. W., *The Biochemistry of Intracellular Parasitism*, The University of Chicago Press, Chicago, 1962, p. 91.

3

RELATIONSHIP TO OTHER LIFE FORMS

Let me begin this last chapter by summarizing what has been learned about metabolic patterns in the psittacosis group. Both DNA and RNA are present, and the whole cycle of multiplication proceeds normally in cell fragments without nuclei. It may, therefore, be concluded that these organisms synthesize their own specific macromolecules of protein and nucleic acid without the intervention of host-made proteins as enzymes or of host-made nucleic acids as templates.

The psittacosis group synthesize a number of low-molecular-weight metabolites that cannot be made by their hosts: folic acid, muramic acid, diaminopimelic acid, lysine, D-alanine, and perhaps still others. These small molecules are clearly the result of parasite activity. How many biosynthetic capabilities the psittacosis group agents possess in common with their hosts is hard to determine, but they must obtain many small molecules by tapping their hosts' free metabolite pools or by digesting their hosts' cytoplasm, as is suggested by electron micrographs of infected cells. The magnitude and structural complexity of the substrate demand of the psittacosis group agents on their hosts may well be such that it cannot be met outside of living cells, and is therefore at least partially responsible for the restriction of these organisms to an intracellular habitat.

The Psittacosis Group as Energy Parasites

The most obvious gap in the metabolic pattern of the psittacosis group is the apparent absence of any energy-generating system. During logarithmic multiplication the generation time is as short as 90 minutes,[1] so they must have ready access to a major source of metabolic energy to maintain such a rapid growth rate. This source is almost certainly oxidative phosphorylation, for when this energy-generating process in infected cells is blocked by anaerobiosis or by inhibitors, multiplication of members of the psittacosis group is also inhibited.[2] Despite this linkage, agent concentrates show no hint of an energy metabolism.[3–5] They do not oxidize pyruvate or the Krebs cycle acids. Glutamate and other amino acids are not oxidatively attacked. There is no oxidation when either oxygen or nicotinamide dinucleotide is used as oxidant. Glucose is not phosphorylated by ATP and is not glycolyzed to lactate. The only oxidative reaction known to be carried out by the psittacosis group is the oxidation of reduced nicotinamide dinucleotide by cytochrome c discovered by Allen and Bovarnick in 1957.[5,6] However, the enzymes which should be on either side of this cytochrome c reductase in the conventional electron transport chain are missing, and the reduction of some unknown oxidant may be the true function of this agent enzyme. Perhaps it is the reduction of folic acid to tetrahydrofolic acid.[6]

The lack of an energy metabolism may be only apparent and the right energy-yielding substrate, present in adequate concentration in vivo, may never yet have been tested in vitro. This explanation cannot be totally refuted because a single positive experiment can undo the conclusions drawn from a hundred negative ones.* However, the finding of Allen and Bovarnick [5] that the conventional electron transport systems are absent make it unlikely, for one is forced into postulating the existence not only of an unusual substrate but also an equally unusual electron transport chain.

To me, it seems more likely that these microorganisms are energy parasites, depending upon their hosts to generate ATP and other high-energy metabolites which they then appropriate to their own biosyntheses. For example, it is possible that they may synthesize their DNA only if supplied with all four deoxyribonucleotide triphosphates, and their protein only if given the proper activated amino acids.

This hypothesis requires that the psittacosis group agents be permeable to compounds that do not pass freely into ordinary intact cells. I believe that there is good evidence that malarial parasites and rickettsiae are unusually permeable to ATP, nicotinamide dinucleotide, and coenzyme A,[7] although Bovarnick,[8] who is responsible for much of the definitive work on this subject, does not entirely agree with me. Smadel [9] has recently suggested that rickettsiae may exhibit exceptional permeability properties which contribute to their obligately intracellular way of life, while Provost, Myers, and Wisseman [10] have shown that typhus rickettsiae have cytoplasmic membranes that are different in important respects from those of bacteria.

* Note added in proof. The single positive experiment may well be the report by Ormsbee and Weiss [*Science,* **142**:1077 (1963)] that the trachoma agent liberates CO_2 from carbon 1 of radioactively labeled glucose.

It may well be that the ability to take up large, complex, and metabolically active molecules is a prerequisite to successful intracellular life. In fact, without this ability, little seems to be gained by living inside a cell instead of outside of it. One can imagine that in the course of adaptation to life inside another cell, an organism may lose many of the active transport systems regulating passage of molecules in both directions across the cell membrane and become permeable to all sorts of molecules which it derives directly from its host. When these molecules come to include the primary sources of metabolic energy, then the ability to generate them may be lost next. This is a testable hypothesis and we can hope that definite answers will soon be available. If it is shown that the psittacosis group are forced to obtain high-energy compounds from their hosts, then this dependency must contribute heavily toward their obligate intracellular parasitism, for only inside living cells would these compounds be present in adequate concentration and variety.

The Psittacosis Group as Bacteria

Since Bedson and his co-workers gave the first comprehensive description of a member of the psittacosis group in the mid 1930's, there have been constant argument and confusion as to whether or not these infectious agents are viruses. Not so many years ago, this situation was understandable, but now is the time to end both the argument and the confusion. Once vague ideas as to the essential nature of viruses have crystallized under the influence of the rapidly increasing knowledge of these entities, and modern concepts of the nature of virus are admirably summarized in the definition of Lwoff (Table 13).[11,12]

The properties of the psittacosis group stand in direct

TABLE 13

Lwoff's Definition of Viruses

"Strictly intracellular and potentially pathogenic entities with an infectious phase:

(a) possessing only one type of nucleic acid;

(b) reproduced from their genetic material and multiplied in the form of their genetic material;

(c) unable to grow and to undergo binary fission, and

(d) devoid of a Lipmann system * "

---

* ". . . . a system of enzymes which convert the potential energy of foodstuffs into the high energy bonds which are needed for biological syntheses. . . . ."

References 11, 12.

opposition to three of Lwoff's four definitive virus characters, and somewhat more obliquely to the fourth.

(a) RNA and DNA are present in almost equal concentrations in both major particle types.

(b) Members of the psittacosis group are not "reproduced from their genetic material and multiplied in the form of their genetic material" because (c) they grow and multiply by binary fission. Study of the multiplication of agents of the psittacosis group with the light microscope has generally led to the conclusion that new particles are formed by binary fission (division of a particle into two approximately equal daughter particles).[13–16] When thin sections of cells infected with these organisms were viewed with the electron microscope, particles in process of binary fission were first observed by Gaylord [17] in 1954 and subsequently seen by many others.[1, 18–23]

Other forms of multiplication have also been reported in the psittacosis group. Budding (unequal division of single particle) and multiple endosporulation (formation of several large particles within a single large one) have been described by Gaylord,[17] Higashi et al.,[18, 19] and Mitsui et al.[21]   Tajima et al.[24] have proposed that new particles are formed by condensations in a structureless matrix, and Higashi et al.[19] and Armstrong et al.[22] have made similar suggestions.   Binary fission, budding, and multiple endosporulation may all be considered special cases of the general reproductive mechanism of fission in which daughter particles arise directly from the cleavage of the parent.   Our group has seen what could be budding particles, but we have never seen structures that might be interpreted as examples of multiple endosporulation.

However, the formation of particles by condensations within a structureless matrix is fundamentally different from fission and may be regarded as a distinctly viral mode of reproduction.   In this laboratory we have never seen structures that could be interpreted in this manner but this, of course, is no proof at all that they do not exist.   However, there are serious objections to the concept of two entirely different mechanisms of reproduction in the psittacosis group.   First, it seems highly improbable that an organism would have two radically different modes of multiplication.   I can think of no well-authenticated parallel. Second, Weiss [25] showed many years ago that penicillin inhibits even the very earliest stages of multiplication of the psittacosis group, which means to me that, at all stages of reproduction, the synthesis of cell wall is involved.   If cell wall is being synthesized, then it is almost certain that multiplication is proceeding by means of some sort of fission.   Strictly speaking, argument as to the occurrence of a mode of reproduction other than fission is immaterial to the question at hand.   Demonstration of reproduction by fission at any stage of the growth cycle is sufficient to put the psittacosis group beyond the pale of viruses.

The position of the psittacosis group with respect to the fourth and final criterion (*d*) is not so clear cut. There is no evidence that they can "convert the potential energy of foodstuffs into high energy bonds," and I have just proposed that these agents depend upon their hosts for the metabolic energy used in biological syntheses. However, when removed from the host cell, some of the psittacosis group can carry out at least one energy-requiring reaction, the sulfonamide-sensitive synthesis of folic acid, presumably from *p*-aminobenzoic acid, glutamic acid, and pteridine (Fig. 15). In this restricted sense at least, the psittacosis group also fail to meet Lwoff's final criterion of virus character.

If these agents are not viruses, then what are they? Some of their nonviral characters, such as the possession of both types of nucleic acids and the presence of folic acid, are universal properties of organisms and are thus of no taxonomic value. Other properties clearly related them to the eubacteria. Table 14 reviews the bacterial properties of the psittacosis group. Their significance has already been discussed. Most of these characters are related to the dem-

TABLE 14

Bacterial Characters of the Psittacosis Group

Morphological characters
    Cell division by binary fission
    Cell surrounded by a rigid cell wall
Chemical characters
    Presence of muramic acid
    Presence of diaminopimelic acid decarboxylase and racemase
    Susceptibility to antibiotics active only against bacteria
    Reversal of D-cycloserine inhibition by D-alanine

onstration in the psittacosis group of structures homologous to the unique cell walls of the eubacteria, specifically to the cell walls of the Gram-negative bacteria.

The assumption that the obligately intracellular members of the psittacosis group have descended from Gram-negative bacterial ancestors capable of living outside of cells and of growing on artificial media poses the unanswerable problem of how this evolution took place. However, unanswerability never stifles speculation; indeed, it often stimulates it. The principle of degenerative or regressive evolution, first clearly formulated by Green [26] and by Laidlaw,[27] is generally used to explain the development of the obligately intracellular parasitic state. The terms "degenerative" and "regressive" are particularly unfortunate and inappropriate as applied here. Obligate intracellular parasites, such as the psittacosis group, the rickettsiae, the malarial parasites, and the viruses, are highly successful, universally distributed organisms in absolutely no danger of extinction. They are exquisitely adapted to their environments and there is no reason to consider them as imperfect organisms or to imply that the evolutionary mechanisms responsible for their development are in any way unusual.

It is seldom recognized that the evolution of an organism capable of growing and multiplying only in another living cell depends upon the operation of two different lines of selection. One line involves the loss of ability to grow extracellularly, and the mechanism here is undoubtedly the occurrence of mutations that reduce the biosynthetic competence of the organism. The other line is concerned with the gain of the ability to survive and multiply within another living cell. Intracellular parasites are often looked down on as metabolic weaklings lacking something required for growth outside of the cells, while few stop to think that their more robust extracellular cousins lack something required for life inside the cell. The ability to grow intracellularly is a highly restricted property among microorganisms, and we know next to nothing of its biochemical basis.

Perhaps intensive study of the facultatively intracellular bacteria, organisms which can grow either in the test tube or in the cell, will in time furnish us with the answers. Evidence is accumulating that the metabolism of bacteria growing inside cells is different from that of the same organisms growing outside. We can hopefully hypothesize that these phenotypic shifts in metabolism have some resemblance to the genotypically fixed alterations in metabolic patterns that give obligate intracellular microorganisms the ability to multiply inside cells and that they may, because of their more superficial character, be more amenable to disclosure. It may even prove possible to shift populations of facultative intracellular parasites from the extracellular metabolic phase to the intracellular one by reconstructing appropriate segments of the intracellular environment outside the cell. In this manner, one could study in vivo metabolism in vitro.

Relation of the Psittacosis Group to Other Small Intracellular Parasites

With the assumption that the microorganisms of the psittacosis group have descended from some remote bacterial ancestor by evolution in an intracellular environment, a lengthy process in which original characters have disappeared and new ones have appeared and become fixed in the genome to give the group its individuality, let us examine other small intracellular parasites for evidence of phylogenetic relationship to the psittacosis group.

Of all the viruses, the pox viruses are most frequently proposed as possible distant relatives of the small intracellular parasites of obvious bacterial lineage, mainly because of their relatively large size and their content of lipids, copper, flavinadenine dinucleotide, and biotin.[28] However, they have other properties which show that their relation to bacteria is exceedingly remote. They contain only DNA and no RNA,[29] they have no muramic acid,[30] their particle envelopes react entirely differently to lipid solvents and enzymes than do bacterial cell walls,[31] and their multiplication is not inhibited by antibacterial drugs.

There has been some speculation that the psittacosis group may be related to the pleuropneumonia-like organisms but this view is no longer tenable, chiefly because the pleuropneumonia-like organisms do not have rigid, muramic acid-containing cell walls and, therefore, are not inhibited by penicillin and other antibiotics whose action is directed against the bacterial cell wall.[32]

In nearly all schemes of classification, the rickettsiae and the psittacosis agents are lumped together in the same taxonomic group. It is true that there are many resemblances between the psittacosis group and the rickettsiae, but they are general ones and may be accounted for by the common bacterial lineage of both. For example, the agents of both meningopneumonitis and typhus rickettsiae have exceptionally small amounts of guanine and cytosine in their DNA's, a property they share with bacteria such as the clostridia.[33] They share no peculiar properties pointing to a recent common origin. Other properties, such as their distinctly different morphologies and the almost invariable occurrence of arthropod vectors in rickettsial diseases and the absence of such vectors in diseases caused by the psittacosis group, argue against any recent divergence from a common stem. There are also deep-seated metabolic differences. Bovarnick and her associates [7] found that rickettsiae aerobically oxidize glutamate with the generation of ATP and have shown that most activities of rickettsiae depend on the constant formation of high-energy phosphate bonds through glutamate oxidation.

It is my guess that continued morphological and biochemical investigation of the variety of small intracellular parasites of vertebrates and arthropods now gathered together in the order *Rickettsiales* will reveal that this taxon harbors many different organisms without recent phylogenetic connection. For example, Suitor, Weiss, and their associates [34-37] have described a small, noncultivatible intracellular parasite of an argasid tick which is structurally and metabolically distinct from either the rickettsiae or the psittacosis group. This organism oxidized both glucose and glutamate, and unlike either rickettsiae or psittacosis group agents was lysed in solutions of low osmotic pressure.

Relation of Different Members of the Psittacosis Group to Each Other

Having looked at the relation of the psittacosis group to other life forms and concluded that they are the not too distant descendants of Gram-negative bacteria, let us now consider the relation of different members of the group to each other. These microorganisms constitute an easily recognizable natural taxonomic group. Their close common ancestry is shown in many ways, most clearly by their practically identical morphology and extensive serological cross-reaction.

Members of the psittacosis group are traditionally divided into avian, mammalian, and human subgroups on the basis of their natural hosts. However, the inadequacy of this method of subdivision is well recognized. For example, some human pneumonitis strains are probably identical with certain strains of avian origin. The use of morphological, biochemical, and serological characters offers a more sensible approach to internal classification of the psittacosis group. Unknown infectious agents may be identified as members of the group if they have the group antigen, while closely related agents may be distinguished on the basis of their specific antigens.

Gordon and Quan [38] have suggested that the psittacosis group may be divided into two natural subgroups on the basis of two characteristics of their inclusion bodies in infected cells, the degree of compactness or diffuseness of the inclusion and the presence or absence of a polysaccharide-containing matrix (Table 15). This iodine and periodic acid-Schiff-positive component of the inclusion was first recognized in the trachoma agent by Rice [39] in 1936, and it was some time before it was realized that the polysaccharide was

TABLE 15

Physiological Subgroups within the Psittacosis Group

Character	Physiological Group	
	A	B
Nature of inclusion		
Morphology	Rigid	Diffuse
Carbohydrate matrix	+	0
Drug susceptibility		
Sulfonamides	+++	0
D-cycloserine	+++	+

Typical members of group A: trachoma, inclusion conjunctivitis, lymphogranuloma venereum, mouse pneumonitis, hamster pneumonitis.

Typical members of group B: psittacosis (most strains), human pneumonitis, feline pneumonitis, meningopneumonitis.

Anomalous agent: psittacosis (strain 6BC).

not restricted to the trachoma inclusions alone but was found in several other members of the group as well. The significance of the presence of a carbohydrate-containing matrix in the inclusion is unknown, but it is obviously not vital to multiplication since many agents grow in inclusions lacking it. It may be formed and excreted by the agent or it may represent an abnormal accumulation by the infected cell. The appearance of the polysaccharide in the trachoma matrix is almost completely inhibited by penicillin,[40] suggesting that it is synthesized by the trachoma agent itself.

The validity of these subgroups is substantiated by the segregation of two other characters in the same manner, susceptibility to sulfonamides [41] and susceptibility to D-cycloserine [42] (H. M. Jenkin, personal communication; F. B. Gordon, personal communication).

The only agent that fails to fit neatly into this scheme is the well-known 6BC strain of psittacosis. It is highly susceptible to sulfonamides and D-cycloserine but does not form a carbohydrate-containing inclusion. However, Dr. R. B. Stewart has informed me that when the 6BC strain is grown in L cells, it forms periodic acid-Schiff-positive inclusions when cortisone is present. No interpretation can be offered for this interesting observation, but it does offer further support for Gordon and Quan's idea of two great natural subgroups.

We may reasonably hope that further work will substantiate, correct, and add to our concepts of the interrelationships among members of the psittacosis group and that there will eventually emerge a binomial system of genera and species that reflects natural relationships. Whatever the nature of the taxon under which these organisms are ultimately gathered, I enthusiastically endorse Meyer's [43] suggestion that the name of Sir Samuel Bedson be reflected in its terminology. Bedson was the first to study these organisms systematically and the first to recognize them as a unique group of infectious agents. To quote Meyer, "The noncommittal use of a proper name is considered preferable (in view of the wide host and tissue range of the members of the group) to a name implying a relationship to a bird genus or to a human disease." To this I add that it is much more euphonious to speak of the bedsoniae than of the psittacosis group or of the currently popular monstrosity, the psittacosis-lymphogranuloma venereum-trachoma group.

To those of you who feel that in this book I have been unduly preoccupied with the distinction between virus and bacterium, I offer this apologia: the distinction is critical. There is an unbridgeable gap between viruses and other infectious agents, and this discontinuity is reflected not only in fundamental differences in the biology and chemistry of the agents themselves but also in the epidemiology, pathogenesis, and therapy of the diseases they produce. Failure to recognize that the bedsoniae are small bacteria and not large viruses can only lead to confusion both in the laboratory and in the clinic. I hope I have convinced you that such confusion is no longer necessary.

REFERENCES

1. Litwin, J., J. E. Officer, A. Brown, and J. W. Moulder, *J. Infectious Diseases,* **109,** 251 (1961).
2. Moulder, J. W., B. R. S. McCormack, and M. K. Itatani, *J. Infectious Diseases,* **93,** 140 (1953).
3. Moulder, J. W., and E. Weiss, *J. Infectious Diseases,* **88,** 56 (1951).
4. Perrin, J., *J. Gen. Microbiol.,* **6,** 143 (1952).
5. Allen, E. G., and M. R. Bovarnick, *J. Exptl. Med.,* **105,** 539 (1957).
6. Allen, E. G., and M. R. Bovarnick, *Ann. N. Y. Acad. Sci.,* **98,** 229 (1962).
7. Moulder, J. W., *The Biochemistry of Intracellular Parasitism,* The University of Chicago Press, Chicago, 1962, p. 55.

8. Bovarnick, M. R., *Ann. N. Y. Acad. Sci.,* **98,** 247 (1962).

9. Smadel, J. E., *Science,* **140,** 153 (1963).

10. Provost, P. J., W. F. Myers, and C. L. Wisseman, Jr., *Bacteriol. Proc.,* p. 133 (1963).

11. Lwoff, A., *J. Gen. Microbiol.,* **17,** 239 (1957).

12. Lwoff, A., in F. M. Burnet, and W. M. Stanley, Editors, *The Viruses,* Academic Press, New York, 1959, Vol. 2, p. 187.

13. Bedson, S. P., and J. O. W. Bland, *Brit. J. Exptl. Pathol.,* **15,** 243 (1934).

14. Bedson, S. P., and J. V. T. Gostling, *Brit. J. Exptl. Pathol.,* **35,** 299 (1954).

15. Swain, R. H. A., *Brit. J. Exptl. Pathol.,* **36,** 507 (1955).

16. Officer, J. E., and A. Brown, *J. Infectious Diseases,* **107,** 283 (1960).

17. Gaylord, W. H., *J. Exptl. Med.,* **100,** 575 (1954).

18. Higashi, N., *Ann. Rept. Inst. Virus Res. Kyoto Univ.* (Ser. B), **2,** 1 (1959).

19. Higashi, N., A. Tamura, and M. Iwanaga, *Ann. N. Y. Acad. Sci.,* **98,** 100 (1962).

20. Litwin, J., *J. Infectious Diseases,* **105,** 129 (1959).

21. Mitsui, Y., M. Kajima, A. Nishimura, and K. Konishi, *Ann. N. Y. Acad. Sci.,* **98,** 131 (1962).

22. Armstrong, J. W., R. C. Valentine and C. Fildes, *J. Gen. Microbiol.,* **30,** 59 (1963).

23. Erlandson, R., and E. G. Allen, *Bacteriol. Proc.,* p. 13 (1962).

24. Tajima, M., Y. Nomura, and Y. Kubota, *J. Bacteriol.,* **74,** 605 (1957).

25. Weiss, E., *J. Infectious Diseases,* **87,** 249 (1950).

26. Green, R. G., *Science,* **82,** 443 (1935).

27. Laidlaw, P. P., *Virus Diseases and Viruses,* Cambridge University Press, London, 1938.

28. Smadel, J. E., and C. L. Hoagland, *Bacteriol. Rev.,* **6,** 79 (1942).

29. Joklik, W. K., *Biochim. Biophys. Acta.,* **61,** 290 (1962).

30. Perkins, H. R., and A. C. Allison, *J. Gen. Microbiol.,* **30,** 469 (1963).

31. Peters, D., *Proc. IV. Intnatl. Conf. Electron Microbiol.* (Berlin, 1958), **2,** 554 (1960).

32. Razin, S., in Klieneberger-Nobel, E., *Pleuropneumonia-Like Organisms (PPLO): Mycoplasmataceae,* Academic Press, London, 1962, p. 91.

33. Belozersky, A. N., and A. S. Spirin, in E. Chargaff, and J. N. Davidson, Editors, *The Nucleic Acids,* Academic Press, New York, 1960, Vol. 3, p. 147.

34. Suitor, E. C., Jr., and E. Weiss, *J. Infectious Diseases,* **108,** 95 (1961).
35. Weiss, E., W. F. Meyers, E. C. Suitor, and E. M. Neptune, Jr., *J. Infectious Diseases,* **110,** 155 (1962).
36. Suitor, E., *Bacteriol. Proc.,* p. 133 (1963).
37. Neptune, E. M., Jr., E. Weiss, J. A. Davis, and E. C. Suitor, *Bacteriol. Proc.,* p. 133 (1963).
38. Gordon, F. B., and A. L. Quan, *Bacteriol. Proc.,* p. 148 (1962).
39. Rice, C. E., *Am. J. Ophthalmol.,* **19,** 1 (1936).
40. Becker, Y., P. Mashiah, and H. Bernkopf, *Nature,* **193,** 271 (1962).
41. Wenner, H. A., *Adv. Virus Res.,* **5,** 40 (1958).
42. Moulder, J. W., D. L. Novosel, and J. E. Officer, *J. Bacteriol.,* **85,** 707 (1963).
43. Meyer, K. M., *Ann. N. Y. Acad. Sci.,* **56,** 545 (1953).

INDEX